SUCCESSFUL
INDEPENDENT
CONSULTING

SUCCESSFUL INDEPENDENT CONSULTING

Turn Your

CAREER EXPERIENCE

Into a Consulting Business

DOUGLAS FLORZAK

LOGICAL DIRECTIONS, INC.
Brookfield, IL 60513

First printing 1999

ISBN 0-9671565-4-8

LCCN 99-72092

ATTENTION CORPORATIONS, UNIVERSITIES, COLLEGES, AND PROFESSIONAL ORGANIZATIONS: Quantity discounts are available on bulk purchases of this book for educational purposes. Special books or book excerpts can also be created to fit specific needs. For information, please contact Logical Directions, Inc., PO Box 0357, Brookfield, Il 60513-0357.

Acknowledgments

An author does not and should not write in a vacuum. Any book worth doing starts with the author's vision and commitment. It's then seasoned with the experience, advice, and inspiration of others. Some people actively participate in shaping the manuscript while others nurture the author's environment. In either case, no author can create a book without their help. I want to thank my reviewers, starting with Chicago-area consultants Candace Masella and Becky Hall. I also want to thank Christopher Juillet from Ann Arbor, Michigan, and Dr. Tom Barker of Texas Tech University for reviewing my manuscript. Chris Juillet's essays on consulting served as an inspiration for some of the material in this book. Tommy's experience with the Society for Technical Communication's (STC) International Special Interest Group on Independent Consulting was very helpful. Thank you all for taking time out from your busy schedules while trying to run your own consulting businesses. I also want to thank my subject matter experts. Mary Micheff of American Family Insurance was very helpful in shaping the chapter on insurance. Larry Hawkins, C.P.A. at Brookfield Financial Plans, Inc., increased the accuracy of chapters dealing with accounting, retirement planning, and record-keeping. Attorney Tom Angell provided valuable input for many of the legal issues covered in this book.

A special thanks goes to my family, starting with my wife, Laurie. Without her continued support, I would have abandoned this project long ago. I also want to thank my sister Robin for her input and encouragement. Credit also goes to my mother and father for never frowning on any creative idea my sister and I presented to them. I also want to thank all my friends from Norwood Street where I grew up. I consider all of them part of my extended family. Finally, I want to thank all the aspiring consultants who asked me about how they could become independent consultants. Their questions, combined with the questions of recently started and even veteran consultants, confirmed the need for a book like this and helped shape its content. I salute you all and hope this book lives up to your expectations.

Contents

Introduction 1

1 *Overview of Consulting* 5

2 *Consulting in Your Field* 19

3 *Drawing From Your Strengths* 27

4 *Creating a Business Plan* 35

5 *Setting Your Rate Structure* 43

6 *The Legal Form of Your Business
and Tax Issues* 55

7 *Insurance* 67

8 *Retirement Funding—The Hidden Benefit* 75

9 *Tips for Setting Up Your Home Office* 83

10 *Marketing Strategies* 91

11 *Interface Materials* 109

12 *Marketing on the Web* 119

13 *Marketing to Agencies* 133

14 *Creating a Marketing Plan* 147

15 *Basic Record-Keeping* 151

16 *Proposals and Contracts* 159

17 *Delivering Your Service* 173

18 *Final Thoughts* 181

Bibliography 185

Recommended Resources 187

Sample Worksheets 201

Index 211

Introduction

"The only books that influence us are those for which we are ready, and which have gone a little farther down our particular path than we have yet got ourselves."

—E. M. Forster (1879–1970), British novelist, essayist
Two Cheers for Democracy, "A Book That Influenced Me" (1951)

There's a reason you picked up this book. Maybe you've just gotten home from a grinding day at work. You're unhappy with the direction your career has taken. The company just finished a round of layoffs. You've survived, but your workload increased because the company has to do the same amount of work with fewer people. Your boss shot down your last 10 suggestions for improving efficiency. You suspect the company isn't finished with layoffs.

Alternatively, perhaps you've just started your consulting business or you're a veteran consultant. You want to know how to promote your Web site. You want more information on setting rates. You're considering incorporation, wondering if this is best for your company. You wonder if you have enough insurance and if your retirement plan is adequate. You want to create a more organized marketing plan.

If you feel tossed by anonymous forces and you seek a chance to become master of your own fate, this book is for you. If you're currently consulting and you want some new ideas, this book is

1

for you. If you're a skilled professional willing to assume the administrative functions of an employer to enjoy the freedom that many employees give up, this book is for you. If you're looking for a road map for running your own business, this book is for you. If you're willing to make a leap of faith, this book is for you.

Why consulting? Unlike a restaurant or retail business, a consulting business is easy to start and requires less money. And, you already have the raw material for the business. You've probably been working in your career for some time, not realizing you are sitting on a potential gold mine. As a "captive employee," you spend all day solving problems and delivering a service for someone else. If you can package your career expertise and you're not afraid to sell yourself, you have what you need to launch a consulting business.

The decision to voluntarily leave a paying job and start a consulting or other business is the most difficult career decision you can make. It's hard to give up "golden handcuffs" such as health insurance, disability insurance, and a retirement plan. Among other things, this book helps you find ways to provide these benefits through your own business with the added advantage of making you the decision maker.

However, not all of us had the option of choosing to quit our jobs to pursue an independent consulting business. Some of us were given a not-so-gentle "push." This is how I started my consulting business. I spent the first few years of my career as a computer programmer working for a large Fortune 500 company. I wanted more experience working with the technology user, so I left my programming job to work for the sales organization of what was then GTE Telenet, providing technical support to the sales force. I didn't know it at the time, but this initial experience with a sales organization exposed me to marketing skills I would need later as an independent consultant. After several years with GTE Telenet, I took another similar job with a sales organization at Wang Laboratories.

Sometime during my five years with Wang, I became disillusioned with the company's entrenched bureaucracy and lack of direction. I started thinking about working for myself. But what kind of consulting business should I start? I considered going back into consulting as a computer programmer, but it had been a long time since I had written computer code. Then, a colleague told me about a friend of hers who was changing careers to technical writing and had enrolled in a college program on the subject. The concept appealed to me. I realized I already spent much of my time at Wang writing technical documents such as proposals and instructions for customers. And I realized I liked this part of the job the most! So, while still working at Wang, I enrolled in a college program on technical communication and started taking classes.

Despite taking these baby steps toward independent consulting, I still resisted the thought of voluntarily quitting my job to start my own business. After all, as much as I disliked my job, it was a known quantity. I figured I would finish my classes, then decide if I liked this new field enough to make the leap into a consulting business. But even as I outlined this plan in my head, I anguished over whether I would have enough moxie to voluntarily give up a "steady" paycheck when decision time came.

Frankly, I'll never know because Wang made the decision for me. I got caught in one of the company's many waves of layoffs during the late 1980s and early 1990s. Suddenly, I was no longer an employee. With a reflex action triggered by fear, I initially looked for another job working for someone else. I attended job fairs and sent out resumes looking for work in both technical sales support and technical writing, but it was during a recession and few companies could match my salary at Wang.

I finally returned to my independent consulting plans. After all, I had nothing to lose. I attended yet another job fair, but this time I passed out a different kind of resume. For the first time in my life, I was selling the services of my own business as a technical writer. Many of the businesses at the job fair were agencies or consulting firms who occasionally subcontracted technical work to independent consultants. Sensing this was the quickest way to get my first contract, I focused on this group.

Although I did not get a contract immediately, I compiled a list of agencies from classified advertisements and did a large mailing of my resume. Finally, I got a response from one consulting company that wanted me to write procedures for one of its clients. I had my first contract! This proved to me that I could successfully market and deliver consulting services. If I could do it once, I could do it again. And so can you.

If you just got laid off from your job or you're working for someone else dreaming of a different career, this book will produce one of two results. If this book provides you with the information you need to finally make the leap, let me be the first to say "welcome." Someday, I hope you will look back, as I often do, and wonder why you hesitated. But if this book convinces you to continue working as an employee, I hope you will not feel you wasted your time. Rather than make assumptions, you were smart enough to research the consulting alternative, weigh the options, and make the decision right for you. Besides, I believe you can still apply some of the information in this book to a career within an entrepreneurial company. Meanwhile, you might want to keep this book in your library, just in case you change your mind.

If you are a newly started or veteran consultant, this book provides some valuable tips and techniques. If you want to save some time, you can skip the first three chapters of this book and focus on the rest. As consultants, we know that we are perpetually learning and if this book adds to your knowledge in some small way, then it's done its job.

While the path to an independent consulting business is long and winding, laden with obstacles, and fraught with fear and doubt, you don't have to go through it alone without a road map. Let this book be your guide.

Overview of Consulting

"In every society some men are born to rule, and some to advise."

—Ralph Waldo Emerson (1803–1882), U.S. essayist, poet, philosopher
"The Young American," lecture, February 7, 1844, delivered to
Mercantile Library Association, Boston (published in
Addresses and Lectures, 1849).

If you are new to consulting, this is your first step. In this chapter, we'll start by trying to define what makes a consultant. Since everyone has a different definition for the practice of "consulting," you'll see it's not easily defined. Why do people become independent consultants? What are the "categories" of consulting? Is there a "career path" for independent consultants? What are the benefits and challenges? This chapter provides answers to these and other questions as it tries to orient you to the world of consulting.

Why do people become independent consultants?

There are many paths that lead to independent consulting. Even if you haven't started your own consulting business, you may be on one of these paths right now and not even realize it! Although the profiles of independent consultants vary, I've identified several scenarios that seem to serve as incubators for people who ultimately become independent consultants. See if any of these apply to you.

"I want to work for myself." Most independent consultants start their businesses because they experience almost an instinctual desire to work for themselves. Are you fed up with the corporate life and all it entails? Do you want more control over your own schedule? Do you believe you can make more money working for yourself? Despite the risks, you may be ready to trade the "security" of a fixed paycheck and provided benefits for the challenge of building a business you can call your own. In today's employment market, working for yourself may be the most stable kind of work. After all, you can't fire yourself!

"I want to release my creativity." Many people feel creatively stifled working for someone else. Unfortunately, many mainstream jobs are not equipped to channel creativity and new ideas from their employees. Are you given the response "that's the way we always do it" after your boss turns down your proposal for an improvement? Does your company have a suggestion box with a lock and no key? Are all your best ideas destroyed by committee?

The desire to express their creativity is one of the driving forces behind many independent consultants. They seek what psychology researcher Dr. Mihaly Csikszentmihalyi calls the "optimal experience" or simply the state of "flow." Csikszentmihalyi defines flow as "the state in which people are so involved in an activity that nothing else seems to matter; the experience itself is so enjoyable that people will do it even at great cost, for the sheer sake of doing it." Does this describe a place you would like to reach?

People tell you, *"I heard you're the expert on this."* Many people become independent consultants as a matter of chance because other people recognize them as experts. Are you the person other employees always come to because you're the only one they know who has experience with a specific type of problem? Are you the only person at your company with skill in a certain operation? Even when given the choice of other employees with similar skills, does management consistently come to you for help? Are you known in your neighborhood as the guy or gal to come to for (you fill in the blank)?

When I was working for a sales branch of Wang Laboratories in the late 1980s, a fellow systems consultant learned the then-new Aldus PageMaker layout computer program. Once sales representatives knew she could create customized marketing materials for their presentations, she was swamped with requests to do this kind of work.

As Wang systems consultants, our primary job was to provide technical assistance to the sales reps and their customers. The situation in this case became so acute the woman complained to her boss that if she tried to fulfill every PageMaker request she received, she would not have time for her other duties! She could easily have started an independent consulting business as a desktop publisher right at that moment.

If you're the person people come to for advice on how to do something in your company or if neighbors and friends come to you, even offering money for your expertise without you asking for it, this may be a sign you were meant to be an independent consultant. If you are lucky enough to be in this situation and recognize it as such, you've already made it past the first hurdle in starting your business because you have an established client base!

"I've been downsized!" No one likes to lose his or her job, but some people use the stimulus of getting laid off to start their consulting business. Sometimes getting laid off can be a blessing in disguise because the decision to cut the "golden handcuffs" of a steady paycheck and provided benefits is extremely difficult for many people. This is how I got started with my consulting business after I was laid off from Wang Laboratories. I felt a combination of shock and betrayal, but relief at the same time. I had been thinking of starting my own business and this forced me to take my dreams seriously.

"I can do this myself, so why am I working for this place?" Many people start a consulting business because they see themselves already doing consulting for someone else. Does your company pay you to provide a service to its customers, charging them a fee for your time? Does your company trust you with important decisions regarding the fate of a client project? Do you sometimes question what "added value" your company provides when it sells

your time to their clients? If you already provide consulting to your employer's clients, it doesn't take long until you realize you can provide the same exact service as an independent consultant to your own clients.

"I want to work in a related field." Many people become consultants because a new development in a related field creates a sudden demand for experts. This situation is particularly prevalent in the technology industry. For example, the demand for Web page designers after 1990 seemed to pop up overnight. How can there be enough experts in a new field that has not been around long enough to produce anyone with experience? The answer lies in consultants with related experience who extrapolate their skills to fill the vacuum. In the case of Web page design, HyperText Markup Language (HTML), its language was similar enough to programming languages for programmers to adopt, and easy enough for visual designers, such as graphic artists, to learn.

What is a consultant?

It's hard to define "consulting" because it applies broadly to many industries. The American Heritage Dictionary defines a consultant as "one that gives expert or professional advice." In his detailed book on the subject, *How to Succeed as an Independent Consultant*, Herman Holtz defined consulting not as a profession in itself, but as a way of practicing a profession in a quasi-professional or technically skilled area for some fixed-fee or rate, on a contract basis. In Janet Ruhl's book, *The Computer Consultant's Guide*, she describes a consultant as someone who takes on higher risk, has more control over their work, and demonstrates greater competence in what they do than the average peer in their industry. In the book *Independent Consulting*, David Kintler states, "Consulting has evolved from being an advice profession to being one more focused on producing results for the client."

Taking all these descriptions into account, I define consulting in terms of two key factors: *experience* and *custom work*. As Janet Ruhl pointed out, to really call yourself a consultant in your field, you must be an *expert*. You must be able to demonstrate that you can provide repeated success for your current clients based on your experience with past clients or a past employer. This means that for most industries, if you are fresh out of college and new to your field, it is difficult to call yourself a consultant unless you can justify that title by showing a record of success outside the classroom. It's not enough to just have a degree or certificate in your field. Even heavily licensed and regulated fields like law and medicine usually include an apprentice period before professionals in those fields "hang out their shingle."

Being an expert in your field also means you must constantly reeducate yourself beyond what is commonly acceptable for your average peers. To communicate competence and earn your client's trust, you must relentlessly enroll in seminars, attend conferences, and scan professional journals for information that will keep you sharp at what you do. Unlike employees, who have a grace period in which they can make mistakes, consultants must hit the ground running when a client hires them.

The other key factor that defines a consultant is the fact that they deliver a custom solution to their clients. This makes consultants specialists in their field. If you build a factory to pump out widgets, the production and sale of widgets is not consulting. But if you take your knowledge of setting up a factory and customize it to show someone else how to build a factory to produce grommets, that's consulting. Generally speaking, the more customized the solution, the more you can charge.

As you develop a consulting business for your field, ask yourself what skills you need to be considered an expert. What professional journals should you read? What organizations should you join? How can you tap your career experience to provide customized solutions for your clients in your industry?

Categories of consulting work

As a consultant, your primary product is your time. You base your proposal to do a project on how long it will take to complete and, as a result, place a value on that time. When you sell your time, the work you're hired to do typically falls into three general

categories: skills contracting, expert-advice consulting, or department-
mental outsourcing.

Skills contracting. Typically, when you start your business, the
easiest kind of work to get and sell to clients is skills contracting.
In a skills contracting scenario, you typically work at the client's
site alongside client employees and/or other consultants and take
direction from the project manager. Because of this fact, some
consultants consider this more like temporary employment than
"true" consulting.

Clients hire independent contractors when they need extra
hands with specific skills to complete a project. Usually, when you
take on this type of work, the client already designed the project
and someone (either the client or a consulting organization hired
by the client) is managing the project. This type of scenario is
prevalent in the technology industry where consultant programmers, technical writers, and testers, among others, fill this niche.

Expert-advice consulting. As you build your reputation and
become more skilled at consulting, you will provide more
expert-advice type consulting. This type of consulting is harder to
sell, but you can charge more for this kind of work. It's easier for
a client to grasp the concept of hiring an additional person to
complete a project that has already started than to convince a
client that you can analyze their operations and make it more
efficient, especially when the client may not know they need this
kind of help. However, if you want to justify charging more for
your time you must add this kind of consulting to your services.

The work you do as an expert-advice consultant usually falls
into one of three types of tasks: analysis, design, or project management. *Analysis* requires you to analyze some aspect of the client's
business and produce a report with your conclusions and suggestions. *Design* work requires you to produce a design report or
prototype others will use as a model to complete projects based
on the design. *Project management* requires you to put together a
team of consultants, or take over the management of an existing
team, to complete a project. It is not unusual for a consultant to
perform all three of these tasks as part of a complete consulting

package offered to the client. You might even perform all three of these tasks when you are the only person on the project.

Departmental outsourcing. As a product of corporate downsizing, many companies eliminate entire departments and outsource the department's services to a separate company that specializes in that particular service. Since duplicating the efforts of a client department is a large task, you might need to hire or subcontract people to provide this service. Your staff may work in the client's building using the client's facilities. For example, many companies specialize in providing computer operations for large corporations. The outsourcing company provides the resources and the outsourcer provides employees to do the work. The outsourcer takes care of payroll, benefits, and training.

Many smaller companies, however, may need only one part-time person to provide the services of an internal department. For example, a medium-sized software publisher decided to outsource their documentation department duties to me when their last technical writer resigned for a position at another company. At that time, they decided one person could handle their documentation requirements on a part-time basis.

What distinguishes outsourcing from other kinds of consulting is that you are not hired for one specific task but to provide appropriate departmental services on demand for a specified period of time. You will probably work onsite, using the resources the client would otherwise provide to its own internal department. This type of work feels the most like working as an employee again since the client typically includes you in departmental meetings and planning sessions.

The three main types of consultants

I've divided the world of consulting roughly into three main types: large consulting organizations, small consulting businesses, and independent consultants.

Large consulting organizations (agencies)

The large consulting organization is any company specifically in the business of providing consultants to its clients from its pool of company or contract consultants. This type of organization usually has a separate sales and recruiting staff that do nothing but find new clients or recruit new consultants for its clients. The owner or owners of the organization are rarely involved in the actual delivery of services. Generally, there are two types of large consulting organizations: temporary agencies that are primarily in the business of providing temporary employees and consulting firms that are primarily in the business of providing solutions to specific client problems or delivering a customized product.

The industry sometimes refers to temporary agencies as "job shops," "employment firms," or "job brokers." Regardless of the title, these companies basically provide temporary employees who supplement the client's regular employees when needed. Clients hire these consultants more for their production skills than for their ability to provide advice to solve a problem. Temporary agencies sometimes maintain permanent employees of their own that they send out on client assignments, but more often than not, they depend on a pool of independent consultants to which they subcontract client work.

The second type of consulting organization is the consulting firm. Large company examples include Andersen Consulting, IBM, and EDI. These companies often maintain a substantial staff of permanent employees occasionally supplemented by contracted consultants. They work either at a client's site or at the firm's own office. These companies usually research a specific client problem and advise on a solution or provide a custom-designed, finished product. For example, the consultants for a computer consulting firm such as IBM, design, code, document, and deliver a custom-designed computer system for its clients. Although they rely heavily on their own staff, consulting firms also often utilize independent consultants, usually to cover areas where their staff is weak. For example, a computer consulting firm that has many programmers on staff may hire independent technical writers to write the documentation for a client project.

For the rest of this book I will generically refer to all large consulting organizations as *agencies*. Chapter 13 discusses agencies in more depth.

Small consulting businesses

A small consulting business is small enough where the owners still actively deliver the services but big enough to subcontract work to independent contractors (consultants) when they have more work than they can handle in-house. They might even have a few full- or part-time employees. In these organizations, the owners might involve themselves in the design and overall project maintenance but subcontract the detail work to someone else.

Independent consultants

Independent consultants are companies made up of one person. They are often referred to as "freelancers," but many consultants don't like to use this term because the word "free" has the psychological implication the consultant doesn't charge for his or her services. Many agencies started as one person and grew as the consultant got more work than he or she could handle alone.

As previously mentioned, many agencies depend heavily on independent consultants and some firms have no consultant employees, subcontracting all their client work to independent consultants. Many independent consultants do all their work through agencies. They are willing to sacrifice some revenue to the agency so they can take advantage of the agency's added marketing resources. In effect, these independent consultants become "wholesale distributors," who sell only to agencies, who in turn market their services to the agency's clients.

Other independent consultants bypass agencies by building a direct client base through their own marketing efforts. This earns them more of the consulting dollar paid by the client, but at the cost of more time spent marketing.

The independent consultant's "career path"

It's hard to identify a common pattern or "career path" successful independent consultants follow. The paths to success are as varied as the consultants themselves. However, I have observed a fairly common growth cycle followed by the owners of many consulting organizations who subcontracted work to me. In this progression, the consultant goes through four phases of growth. I identify these phases as contractor, independent consultant, small consulting business owner, and large consulting firm owner. You may not decide to follow this path exactly, but it demonstrates some of your options.

Contractor

This is where most consultants start out. In this phase, you need to quickly build your portfolio of work and word-of-mouth awareness with potential clients. The quickest way to do this is to initially subcontract work from agencies as a W-2, temporary employee while building your own direct client base. Some consultants are able to bypass the subcontracting route and develop their own direct clients immediately. In either case, the type of work you most often do in this phase is production-skill work because this work is most in demand.

Independent consultant

In this second phase, you've worked in your field as a consultant for some time and you've developed enough direct clients that · subcontracting from agencies becomes a smaller and smaller percentage of your business. You're doing more expert-advice consulting, such as design and analysis, for a higher contract rate. You're starting to look more like a "real" business. Rather than let agencies do the marketing for you, you're doing more direct marketing.

Small consulting business owner

In this phase, your marketing efforts hit a critical mass where you're so busy you have to turn away a significant amount of business. As a consummate entrepreneur, this frustrates you. You can continue establishing your reputation and charging more for your time. The drawback is that every field responds to basic price elasticity at some point, above which you simply cannot increase your rate. Many consultants content themselves with this upper "ceiling" and just continue what they are doing while enjoying the relatively unencumbered lifestyle that accompanies independent consulting. If you see this as a business opportunity, however, rather than turn business away, you decide to spread out. You hire subcontractors to do much of the detail work while you focus on design, project management, and marketing. You're still directly involved with the completion of client projects, but you're not trying to do it all yourself. While this increases your risk and complexity, it also enables you take on larger projects.

Large consulting organization owner

As your small consulting business continues to grow, the demand on your business requires that you spend more time strategizing the direction of your company than personally delivering services. Your company is experiencing growing pains. You've decided to make the leap into the big leagues. You hire professional marketing and sales reps to take over those functions. You continue to subcontract independent consultants to deliver your services, but now you have enough work to start hiring full-time consultant employees. To fund all this, you might apply for a bank loan or solicit partners or investors. Now you're competing with large agencies and consulting firms such as CARA, Manpower, and Renaissance Worldwide.

Benefits of consulting

The consulting lifestyle offers many benefits. Here are some examples.

You are not dependent on one employer. Corporate "downsizing" doesn't bother you because if work dries up with one client, you can find another client who will take up the slack. Also, unlike an employee, you are not stuck with only one company's view of the world. By working with different clients you see many different corporate cultures, providing you with a valuable perspective that benefits yourself and your clients.

You choose your own projects. Many people seek control and diversity in their work. Unlike employees, you can turn down work you don't want to do and select projects that interest you. This not only appeals to your need for diversity, but it expands your experience.

You have more control over your schedule. Depending on your field, your consulting work may allow you to work at home. Provided service to your client doesn't suffer, you can adjust your hours to work when you are most productive. If you do your best work from 8 PM to midnight, you can work then, or you can complete a project over the weekend. This could free a weekday to complete errands during nonpeak periods while the rest of the world is at the office.

You set your own income goals. A raise in your income is not tied to your next review. You decide if you want to be aggressive and take on a lot of work or cut back and spend more time on other things. To diversify your income, you can branch out into other related businesses without being accused of "moonlighting."

You avoid some office politics. Most of the time, you can focus on your work because you are not competing with other employees for promotions. However, company politics can still affect you. For example, occasionally certain forces within a project may attempt to shift the blame for a failed project from themselves to you, the outside consultant.

You control your retirement investments. This is an often overlooked advantage. Many employees are not pleased with the limited choices their employers provide them for investing their 401(k) retirement savings. As a self-employed person, you determine exactly how and where you want to invest your retirement funds.

Challenges to consulting

Like any career option, consulting includes several challenges that stretch you financially, mentally, and spiritually. However, the process of meeting and overcoming these challenges strengthens your business and builds character.

You must purchase your own benefits. As a business owner, you bear the burden of providing benefits to your employees (that's you!) On the one hand, you probably have to purchase these benefits at higher cost than your previous employer. On the other hand, as with your retirement investments, you may have more control over the type of benefits you select.

You may not make your income goals. There is no guarantee you will generate the income you expect. After you set your revenue goals, you have to get the work and after you get the work there is no guarantee the client will pay you. If you don't control your costs, there is no guarantee you will make a profit.

You must do everything yourself. When the telephone rings, you become the receptionist. When you need more clients, you become the salesperson. When you pay yourself, you become the company treasurer. When you need to load software, you become the system administrator. You must provide all these support activities and still have time to deliver services to clients!

You often feel isolated. I know more than one successful consultant who went back to captive employment because he or she missed the social interaction among the "water cooler community" that pops up at most large organizations. If you work at home, you feel particularly isolated. You can offset this somewhat by planning lunch meetings with friends or peers and attending professional meetings. Even if you work on a client site, you often cannot establish long-term relationships because, just as you get settled in, the project ends and you move on.

You do not have a well-defined "career path." Some companies have well-defined steps on the ladder to success. For example most of the top 10 accounting firms have specific steps that an employee can follow toward becoming a full partner in the business. If you desire a career with a "planned" path, consulting may not be for you. As mythologist Joseph Campbell once asked, "What if you get to the top of your ladder to success and discover that it's against the wrong wall?"

Consulting
in Your Field

"People don't choose their careers; they are engulfed by them."

—John Dos Passos (1896–1970), U.S. novelist
New York Times (October 25, 1959)

To give your consulting business the best chance for success, you should assess your field to learn who your clients are and how well your field supports consultants. For example, why do clients in your field seek consultants? Will you consult to business, consumers, or other consultants? Are there any professional organizations for consultants in your field? Answering these and other questions about your field before you start consulting will provide the background you need to shape your business.

Why do clients need consultants?

As part of your research you should know why clients in your industry hire consultants. Some common reasons follow.

Their problem is highly specialized. Most clients hire consultants because they do not have the talent in-house to solve a particular problem. Clients are willing to pay a consultant if they believe the consultant can help them avoid "reinventing the wheel."

They cannot complete their project on time without help. One effect of corporate downsizing is that many companies face the same deadlines with fewer resources. The only way they can complete projects on time is to outsource some of the work. This

19

primarily benefits skills contracting but even expert-advice consultants can benefit from this client problem by accelerating the design and analysis phase of a project.

They want to save money on employee benefits and payroll taxes. Another product of the corporate "right-sizing" paradigm is the drive for companies to maintain the absolute minimum headcount. By hiring a consultant to "fill in the gaps" when they need him or her rather than developing the same talent in-house, clients minimize the cost of employee benefits and payroll taxes. Even though a client will pay a consultant more per hour than their employees and some consulting projects run for years, clients still feel they save money over the long-term. They also avoid the hiring/layoff cycle that occurs as the company's fortunes expand and contract during its business cycle.

They can't find enough qualified professionals. Many industries have grown so rapidly that they have a shortage of skilled professionals. This is particularly true in the computer technology industry where many trade papers cite the shortage of programmers, testers, technical writers, and trainers. While this increases the salaries clients offer for permanent employees, it also increases the demand for consultants.

They need to get an objective opinion. Sometimes clients hire consultants to avoid potential bias from an analysis conducted by internal personnel. A client may hire a consultant to help him or her choose between solutions proposed by different vendors. Unfortunately, many clients take the advice from consultants more seriously than the same advice they receive from their employees. There have even been cases of frustrated employees quitting to start their own consulting business, only to have their former employer hire them back to provide the same advice they were trying to offer as employees!

They need information from an "insider." Some clients hire consultants specifically because the consultants had an experience or previous job that gives them a special insight. For example, many computer security specialists sought Clifford Stoll's advice after he discovered a computer hacker at Lawrence Berkeley Lab, as detailed in his book, *The Cuckoo's Egg*. This type of expert-advice consulting is also common among ex-government employees. For example, many White House advisors become consultants after they leave the Capitol, and many military personnel become consultants to the armaments industry after they retire. Clients hiring these kinds of consultants seek inside information that will help them market to or influence the decisions of people in the consultant's field.

They need a licensed professional. Many companies cannot afford to maintain licensed professionals such as attorneys, doctors, or accountants on staff, so they hire these professionals as consultants when they need them. Clients may also seek to hire consultants certified on particular products so they can maintain warranties or work closely with the product vendors.

They need to certify their product. Some clients need consultants to help them meet a specific certification process. For example, ISO 9000 is a set of international guidelines intended to evaluate a company's ability to respond to quality issues. Some companies, particularly in Europe, require their vendors to be ISO 9000 compliant. Shortly after ISO 9000 was adopted, consultants started offering services intended to help clients meet ISO 9000 certification.

Types of consulting clients

Who will need your consulting experience in your field? There are three basic types of clients: business, peers, and consumers. Each type of client requires a different marketing strategy. In your field, you may market to only one type or to all three.

Consulting to business

Most people looking to leverage their career experience end up doing business-to-business consulting. Business consulting projects tend to be more specialized and last longer than consumer consulting projects. A brief list of examples includes:

> Architects
> Corporate trainers
> Data processing operators
> Efficiency experts
> Engineers

> Freelance writers
> Graphic artists
> Indexers
> Office organizers
> Programmers
> Software testers
> Software usability experts
> Technical writers

Consulting to peers

Either by objective or because of your extensive industry experience, at some point you may become a consultant to peers in your field. Almost every field has consultants who offer to help others in their field get started or improve their skills in a particular discipline. These consultants usually provide these services through seminars and/or publications, but some even offer individual mentoring services.

If you intend to do peer consulting, the best services to offer are any that help professionals in your field enhance their credentials. This can include seminars to help someone in your field pass a required certification process. You can also provide advice on how to become an independent consultant in your field. Of course, this requires that you successfully run your consulting business for some years before you start advising someone else. Even in the early stages of your consulting business, don't be surprised if you get questions from employees and friends about *how you got started*. Many people often dream of starting their own business and are willing to pay an expert for advice on *how to begin*.

Consulting to consumers

If your area of expertise makes you an expert in providing consulting to the average person, you are marketing to consumers. Traditional professions such as accounting, law, and medicine fall into this category. It also includes some less obvious professionals:

> Banquet planners
> Career counselors
> Education counselors

Financial aid consultants
Financial planners
Marriage counselors
Matchmakers
Personal shoppers
Wedding planners

This is a very short list, but each of these consultants markets to consumers. Most consultants who market to consumers tend to have more clients than those who market to business. This is because a business consulting project can last months whereas consumer consultants tend to complete their work in a much shorter time.

Good consumer consultants generate a large demand for their time, usually based on strong word-of-mouth from satisfied clients. As the demand for their time increases, so does their rate. But, as mentioned earlier, there is usually a limit on how high you can raise your rate for your time in response to increased demand. As a result, many consumer consultants turn to other means to distribute expert advice, including newsletters, books, tapes, and seminars. Some consumer consultants even start their business from this point. For example, Amy Dacyczyn became an expert on traditional and nontraditional ways for the everyday person to save money through frugal living. She publishes *The Tightwad Gazette* newsletter and has authored three successful books on the subject. She has become such an expert in her field, national television shows and newspapers often seek her for interviews.

Assessing your field

The potential success of a consulting business in your field depends on several factors.

Complexity of your work

The success of a consulting business in your field depends on its level of complexity. Typically, the more complex the work, the greater the demand for consultants. Is there a shortage of skilled professionals in your field? This will increase the demand for all kinds of professionals, employees, and consultants.

Availability of agencies

If your field has third-party companies providing consultants and/or contingent workers, it's a sure sign that your field has a thriving consulting channel. The best way to see the extent of agencies servicing your field in your area is to check the employment pages of your local newspaper. Look for ads by consulting companies offering to hire full-time or contract consultants.

Samples of your work

Does your work allow you to provide samples of a completed project? Most graphic artists and technical writers, for example, are expected to provide samples of their work to potential clients. The advantage of doing consulting in a field that provides samples is that you can show a potential client tangible results of a similar project. When you begin your consulting business, you won't have samples from consulting projects. You may be able to draw from samples of work you've done from your employers—provided you get their permission.

Licensing

If your field requires or supports any type of licensing or certification, this is a sign that the profession has matured. This increases the chances for a successful consulting business in your field. Some, such as accounting, law, and medicine require licensed practitioners. Other fields offer certifications that may not be required but could enhance your credentials. For example, the data processing industry provides a certification program and many product vendors provide certification programs for their products.

Professional organizations

Another sign of a mature field is one that includes professional organizations. These organizations are dedicated to educating their members and the industry about issues concerning their field. For example, doctors have the American Medical Association (AMA); lawyers have the American Bar Association (ABA); and my field of technical communication has the Society for Technical Communication (STC). If your field is too new to have a professional organization, you might want to consider starting one with other professionals.

Professional organizations provide the following benefits.

Source of clients. Professional organizations can be the best source of clients for your business. Members of the organization already understand your business and may have heard about you from other members.

Networking with colleagues. These organizations provide the best place to network and build relationships with other professionals in your field. This pays dividends when colleagues refer work to you and tip you off to new tools or developments in your field. As mentioned earlier, networking also reduces the sense of isolation that can accompany independent consulting. You can network by mingling with other members at meetings. If you want a higher profile in the organization, you can volunteer for organization duties or run for office.

Inexpensive advertising. Most professional organizations include a directory of members. This is one of your best sources of advertising. Besides distributing them to members, the organization often provides directories to potential clients, and agencies often use them to recruit contract consultants. Many organizations also allow you to purchase their mailing list.

Publications. Most organizations publish a newsletter and/or journal. In addition to providing information about your field, these publications provide valuable information for independent consultants. Many organizations accept advertising in their publications. This allows you to scan the publications for ads by agencies and to place your own ads.

Programs and training. Professional organizations usually provide monthly programs and special seminars. Some also provide formal classroom training for professionals in their field. This is a relatively inexpensive way to stay current on tools and techniques in your field.

Independent consultant support. Some professional organizations are specially designed by and for independent consultants. For instance, the Independent Computer Consultants Association (ICCA) is an organization made up exclusively of independent consultants and agencies in the computer industry. Others, like the STC, operate Special Interest Groups (SIGs) for independent consultants. These specialized organizations offer consolidated resources for independent consultants. Some publish their own directories and operate telephone or online bulletin boards intended to match independent consultants with client projects.

Published industry statistics. Usually, one of the functions of an industry organization is to collect and publish statistics about its membership and the industry in which it operates. This can provide a wealth of information about potential clients. Some organizations that accommodate independent consultants collect statistics on consulting rates that can help you determine your own rate.

Industry publications

Another way to measure the consulting potential of your field is to view industry or "trade" publications. Most mature industries not only produce periodicals from professional organizations but for-profit magazines and newsletters. You can scan these periodicals for clues to new niches you can fill with your consulting business. You can also check these publications for ads from agencies or other independent consultants.

Complementary fields

Evaluate your field for any complementary fields. For instance, my field of technical communication is closely related to other fields such as software development, training, and indexing. Analyze each of these related fields for professional organizations and industry publications. Some of these may provide crossover marketing opportunities. You may decide to join the professional organizations of a related field or subscribe to some of its periodicals. You could also negotiate a referral system with professionals in related fields to increase your exposure.

Drawing From Your Strengths

"I have only got down on to paper, really, three types of people: the person I think I am, the people who irritate me, and the people I'd like to be."
—E. M. Forster (1879–1970), British novelist, essayist
Address to PEN Club Congress, quoted in
"Huw Weldon," *Monitor* (1962)

To become a successful independent consultant, you draw on skills, traits, and experience developed throughout your career. Depending on your career history, some of these things transition easily to consulting and some require work. One of the exciting things about consulting is discovering a skill or trait you took for granted in your job as an employee and applying it as an entrepreneur.

As you assess the skills and traits that provide the tools and character you need to survive as a consultant, you also need to assess your qualifications. This includes your experience, education, certifications, and professional memberships. Since the business of consulting is selling yourself, you must know how to get the most benefit from your qualifications.

Traits of successful independent consultants

What personality traits make a successful consultant? Opinions vary, but I think you can cope with independent consulting if you exhibit the following traits.

You write and speak well

Regardless of your field, you must be a good communicator, which means you must be a good writer and speaker. In most consulting situations the main output of your business is written material. This includes your own marketing materials as well as analysis reports for your clients. As a consultant, you will often make oral presentations to your clients explaining your findings or providing training.

You listen to others

Although excellent written and verbal skills provide the key "outputs" of your business, good listening skills provide the essential "inputs." You must be a good listener to properly qualify your clients and to understand their business problems.

You're not afraid to sell yourself

As a one-person business, you cannot be afraid to sell yourself. Many people have a natural fear of promoting themselves because they were taught not to "brag," but proper marketing is not bragging. If you don't get the word out about your business, how will your clients find you?

You're a good problem solver

Clients hire you to help them solve their problems. As a successful consultant, you must be part detective, part scientist, and part plumber. This is true whether you are doing skills or expert-advice type consulting.

As a detective, you must constantly ask questions and probe for clues that point to a cause of and potential solution to a problem. One way you apply this in skills contracting is when you uncover problems that interrupt the production process. Captive employees may be content to take production down time as a cue for a coffee break while they wait for "others" to solve the problem, but you will try to find a solution to the problem. For expert-advice type consulting, your detective work compels you to interview company experts and examine company documents in search of clues.

As a scientist, you conduct experiments to test your theories. For skills contracting, this means testing components of your work to see if they function properly. For example, a programmer will repetitively run and test code. For expert-advice consulting, you may apply statistical sampling as your scientific tool, such as a questionnaire to collect organizational information to support your conclusions.

Finally, as a plumber, you know how to put the pieces together in the right order and take into account the impact on the total system or organization. For skills contracting, this means knowing who supplies you the pieces that feed your work and who receives the product of your work. It also means you constantly review this process and propose improvements. For expert-advice consulting, you must take into account the big picture and analyze how your solution will impact all parts of the organization.

You're self-motivating and self-managing

As an independent consultant, you can't wait for someone to tell you what to do. You have to know how to manage yourself. As experienced consultant Candace Masella explains, "Over the years I have hired people who were cut from a company payroll even though they were in good standing with the company. However, what some of these folks lacked was the ability to work without supervision. They really needed direction and affirmation from a 'boss.' The abilities to be self-motivating and self-managing are absolutely essential qualities for the independent. If they lack these, I would suggest they do not try consulting."

You accept relentless change

While the world in general seems to change faster than before, the world of consulting changes even faster. To maintain your expert status you must stay current on developments in your field. This is particularly true with consulting in any technical industry. You must consume trade publications, seminars, and support tools. If your consulting practice is very specialized and tied to a vertical market, you must be ready to move with changes in that market.

This also applies when you're in the client's work environment. You must have the flexibility to "roll with the punches" by adapting to limited resources and changing project requirements.

As an independent consultant, however, you have many advantages. Because you are smaller, you can adapt to change more rapidly than large organizations. Its easier for you to extrapolate skills and retrain yourself when necessary to accommodate changes in your industry. On the other hand, although it is easier for you to make the decision to move in another direction, you have fewer resources than larger organizations.

You learn quickly

Unlike captive employees who can participate in planned company training programs, independent consultants must learn on the fly. By definition, since you are providing a custom solution, your clients cannot expect to hire someone who instantly knows everything about their individual situation. But they do expect you to learn about their business quickly and leverage past experience with similar clients to solve their problem.

For skills contracting this presents a problem. Your clients will expect you to be operational with the appropriate production tools, but your industry may have many tool vendors. You can't be proficient with them all. One way around this is to convince your client that you can extrapolate your knowledge of similar tools to quickly learn corresponding functions on their tools. For example, most technical writers work well with at least one word processing program. Because most operating systems now force developers to adopt standard interfaces, most word processing software has the same features and functions. Most independent technical writers know how to find similar functions in a new word processor. This is usually less of a problem for expert-advice consulting because the final product is typically a report and/or presentation and clients usually don't care what tool you used to produce your work.

You manage money well

As an independent consultant, you are also a business owner. You need to manage your cash flow and expenditures as any other business would. Even if you hire an accountant or bookkeeper to handle the finances of your business, you still need to understand basic bookkeeping so you can manage your business.

You know your limits

As an independent consultant with limited resources, it's as important to know what you *can't do* as it is to know what you *can do*. In their desperation to complete a project, some clients may want to hire you when you know you don't have the appropriate level of skills to handle the complexity of the project. Another potential trap is when you're tempted to take on more work than you can realistically schedule.

You cannot afford to risk your reputation by taking on work that is over your head or by overbooking your time, so you must be good at judging when to walk away from a client's project. You can still help the client by recommending another consultant who has the skills the client needs. When you do this the client will respect your honesty and consider you for other projects.

Your qualifications

To sell yourself as a consultant you must sell your qualifications. Since consulting varies from field-to-field, how do you build your qualifications? The following qualifications are common to many fields of consulting.

Years of experience

As stated earlier, you must be an expert to be a consultant in your field. The best way to communicate your expert status is through your years of experience. When you consider your years of experience, include time worked in areas related to the field in which you will market your services. For example, in my field of technical communication, I not only have many years as a technical writer, but more than a decade as a programmer. Since most of the projects I work on involve writing documentation for computer systems, my experience as a programmer is relevant.

Education

If you have any degrees in the particular industry for which you are consulting, it adds to your qualifications. But, as with years of experience, related degrees count. If you decide to consult as an industrial trainer, a degree in psychology would probably be relevant. If you feel your current educational background does not enhance your qualifications and your field is weighted heavily toward consultants with the proper education, you may consider enrolling in a degree program relevant to your field.

The time and expense involved make it difficult to obtain an advanced degree. Fortunately, many fields provide shortened versions of fully advanced degrees. I was able to shore up my technical writing skills by taking a 17-hour certificate program in technical and professional communications at the Illinois Institute of Technology.

Certifications

In some fields, such as medicine, law, or accounting, you cannot even practice without the proper certification. In many other fields, although certification isn't technically required, it becomes the "coin of the realm." For instance, if you intend to consult on computer network installation, you should become a Certified Network Engineer (CNE) in Novell or Microsoft networking products.

Although certification isn't required in most fields, it enhances your qualifications. Many certification programs are either tied to an industry professional organization or particular industry products. Choosing the proper product certification can be a key part of your overall marketing plan, and in most cases, completing a product certification program is quicker and less expensive than enrolling in an advanced degree program at a university.

Microsoft, for example, maintains an extensive certified professional program for all its major products and provides limited marketing for its consultants. When you become a Microsoft certified consultant, you earn the right to display the Microsoft certified consultant logo on your business card. This can be quite a selling point if you are marketing to Microsoft users. Many other technology products also provide certification programs particularly for consultants who train users in their product. Other examples from the software industry include Quark, Adobe, and Power Builder.

It isn't just the technology field that provides certification programs. Many other fields have their own professional organizations or products that sponsor certification programs. Next time you see a business card or advertisement for someone offering consulting services in your field, look for any certification logos and find out what the requirements are to get certified. The Recommended Resources section of this book contains references for several books on getting product certifications.

Professional memberships

Besides providing "insider" information and interaction with your peers, professional memberships also enhance your qualifications. Professional memberships communicate that you are serious about your profession. In some fields clients expect you to be a member of the appropriate professional organization. Most doctors are members of the American Medical Association (AMA) and most lawyers are members of the American Bar Association (ABA).

Quality measures

Quality measures are any objective third-party endorsements of your work. This includes industry awards, client testimonials, or trade paper reviews. Any time you can add this kind of publicity to your marketing materials, it adds to your industry qualifications. Industry awards in particular can help distinguish you from your competition, particularly in a field where clients have trouble judging the difference between good and bad practitioners. For example, in my field of technical communication, many clients have trouble judging the nuances of good and bad documentation. Fortunately, every year the Society for Technical Communication sponsors a technical publication competition. Being an "award winner" in any field is a concept any client can understand and one that differentiates you from your competition.

Creating a Business Plan

"You can never plan the future by the past."
—Edmond Burke (1890–1969), Irish-born British politician and writer

If you read enough books about starting a business, you will repeatedly encounter authors advising you to create a written business plan beforehand. This is good advice, although I know many consultants (including myself) who started their business without one, yet went on to run a thriving business. Perhaps these businesses would have reached success earlier if they had used a business plan. Since starting my business, I began using a business plan as a tool to refocus my efforts. So, in a case of "do what I say, not what I did," I recommend you create a business plan early on.

What is a business plan used for?

There are two potential uses for a business plan. The first, and more traditional purpose, is to gain financing for the business. Financing can come in the form of investors buying shares or banks lending the business money to grow. If you were a potential investor risking your own money or a banker putting your bank's money on the line, you would want to know everything you could about the business that was going to spend the money, right? In these cases, the business plan demonstrates your competence, shows how you'll spend the money, and tries to assure the lenders they'll get rewarded for taking a risk on you.

The second use for a business plan is as a strategic planning tool to guide the direction of your business. Since most single-person consulting companies run a low-overhead business and rarely seek outside funding, this is the best use of a business plan for the independent consultant, particularly in the startup phase. In this case a written business plan helps you maintain your focus. After you develop your initial written business plan, you should review it every year and make adjustments as necessary for the year ahead. If you follow this practice, you can include your yearly marketing plan as part of the overall annual plan.

Components of a business plan

What you put into your business plan depends on the audience. When you write your business plan, I suggest you visualize a mythical group of investors or board of directors to which you must present this information. Even though you are probably just a one-person business right now, it's all right to use the word "we" when writing your business plan. It will make you feel like a bigger business and if you're used to accomplishing your goals as part of a team, it may make it easier to visualize your plans.

The Worksheet section at the end of this book contains a worksheet to get you started on your own business plan. It includes the following sections:

Mission statement. The primary purpose of a mission statement is to provide a vision for your business congruent with your personal goals. It answers the question "who am I?" The best mission statement is one that isn't too specific. You should consider it a general guide rather than a detailed plan. Each day you'll interpret how you'll execute your mission statement.

Strategy. This is where you summarize your business strategy. Point out any unique skills, experience, and knowledge you offer. Touch on how you will distinguish your business from your competition and how you will connect with the market.

Current status and future plans. Use this section to describe the current state of your business and what you plan to accomplish in the near term. If you seek investment or funding from an outside source, briefly explain how you would use the money to grow your business. If you are not seeking capital, mention how you intend to continue funding the business (personal loan from yourself, from business revenues, credit cards, and so forth).

Market analysis. Here you summarize the current market conditions for your industry. Analyze whether the market is expanding or contracting and whether this is a healthy environment for your business. A contracting market is not necessarily bad for your business if you provide services that help your clients cope with a shrinking market. If possible, cite statistics to quantify the market's size and potential.

Market niche. In this section you zero in on the part of the market that offers the best opportunity for your business. Describe the unique nature of each market segment you intend to approach and the type of service you intend to deliver.

Client profile. Use this section to describe your typical client. Profile your clients and visualize how they do their job. Identify how they choose an outside consultant and where they typically look for them.

Main features and benefits. Use this section to elaborate on the core features of your service and the benefits these services bring to your clients. Point out how your services differentiate you from your competition.

Competitive analysis. When you analyze your competition, provide an overview of the competition and the competitive environment in which your business operates. If appropriate, pick out individual companies against which you expect to compete. Then, discuss the strengths and weaknesses of your business against the competition. Try to realistically identify the direct or indirect threats (if any) that face your business. This prepares you to answer questions posed by your target clients while they consider you against your competition.

Marketing plan. Explain how you plan to "get the word out" about your business. Describe your plan to use networking, word-of-mouth, advertising, telemarketing, direct mail, publicity, and any other marketing techniques. Try to demonstrate why you chose one marketing device over another.

Professional assets. Provide a short biography about yourself and any other key people in your business, including background and professional memberships. You might even include biographies about outside professionals employed by your business, such as an accountant or attorney. This section is particularly important if you intend to use your business plan to attract outside funding. People are the foundation of a consulting business, and you will have to convince the money suppliers that you are equipped to succeed.

Projected cash flow. Projected cash flow is a financial form that estimates how much money the business will make and how much it will spend over a twelve-month and/or multi-year period. This is the most difficult part of a business plan because it is the most quantifiable and the most obvious if you don't meet your projections. Hence, you should be conservative about your potential revenue and realistic about your expenses.

The sample business plan shown does not contain a projected cash flow. A Cash Flow worksheet is provided in the Worksheet section at the end of this book.

Business Plan for TWrite, Inc.

Mission Statement

The goal of this business is to...

- Provide creative solutions to clients with a focus on documentation, training, and programming.
- Advise clients on the most appropriate solution for their business problems.
- Stay current and maintain a high skill level by continually investing in the best professional development and training this business can afford.
- Continually develop complementary products and services.

Strategy

TWrite, Inc. provides professional consulting for technical publications. This includes documentation, instructional design, and document automation through programming.

The document automation part of the business supports the other two by providing labor-saving, proprietary macros and programs that accelerate the development of documentation and/or training materials. This key component of the strategy differentiates us from the competition.

The other key strength of the business is the staff at TWrite. Our goal is to combine the art of communication with the science of technology. We continue to invest in both our technical knowledge and communication skills. This helps to differentiate us from other consulting firms that focus primarily on technical expertise, as in the case of a software consulting company, and those that focus primarily on written and visual communication skills, such as a graphic arts or marketing consulting company.

TWrite will rely primarily on word-of-mouth and networking to connect with its target market. The company will also engage in some direct telephone sales, direct mail, and limited advertising in (primarily local) trade publications.

12/16/98   ■ 1

Figure 4-1: Sample business plan

Current Status & Future Plans

The company has been in business for several months now with mixed success. We do most of our business with direct clients, but still occasionally subcontract with larger consulting companies. We have a few clients that provide repeat business, and many one-time clients.

In the near term, we need to improve our repeat business and increase our marketing efforts to add new clients. We need to improve our knowledge and credentials in instructional design and Visual Basic programming. We need to improve our skills in HTML, HTML Help, and JavaScript.

Initial funding for the business was provided by the President, George Conrad. For the near term, the business intends to continue funding its operations from its revenues without seeking outside financing.

Market Analysis

The demand for technical communication services should continue to provide a healthy environment for TWrite. One example of the increase in demand for technical communication professionals is the fact that between 1994 and 1998, membership in the Society for Technical Communication (STC) increased 24% from 16,331 to 20,190 members. The need for technical communication and training continues to expand due to rapid developments in computer technology and increased global competition.

The rapid advance of computer technology creates a constant stream of new software and hardware. This continues to create a demand for new and updated documentation and training by both the technology vendor and the technology consumer.

Increased global competition pressures companies to get their employees productive quickly. This increases the demand for documentation and training materials that can successfully get employees up and running with a minimum of down time.

Niche

TWrite intends to focus on documentation and instructional design with an emphasis on electronic delivery of products produced by these services.

The documentation part of the business will focus on providing paper and online documentation for software products. The target client for this type of service are companies developing software. This includes software manufacturers developing software for commercial distribution and medium to large companies developing software for internal use.

The instructional design part of the business will focus on developing materials for classroom and online delivery of business training. The target client for this type of service is the training or marketing department of medium to large companies.

Figure 4-1 (continued)

Client Profile

Clients for documentation services tend to be small to large companies who have the resources to budget for the design and production of documentation for their software products. This includes software for sale or proprietary software intended for the company's own employees.

The decision maker for our clients typically require outside help when they've fully tapped their internal resources and cannot complete the documentation for a project on time without outside assistance. They base their decision to hire outside documentation consultants primarily on price, availability, and experience. They find consultants through word-of-mouth, professional organizations, directories, and occasionally from advertisements in (primarily local) trade publications.

Main Features & Benefits

The two key features of TWrite is the technical background and training of its staff and the ability to automate documents through macros and other proprietary programming methods. This benefits clients by providing a higher level of technical expertise than that provided by the average technical communicator coming from a non-technical discipline. Additionally, development of proprietary macros and other programs to automate creation of documents benefits clients by accelerating development of client materials.

Competitive Analysis

Overview

The competition for TWrite includes independent consultants and larger consulting organizations. Independent consultants are typically single person businesses that specialize in technical communication. Based on participation in the local Society for Technical Communication (STC), there are anywhere from 50–100 independent consultants operating in the area. Many of these work exclusively through agencies and larger consulting firms as subcontractors while a smaller minority actively market to their own client base.

There is a plethora of large consulting organizations that operate in the area. Most of these companies are either temporary agencies or solution developers. The temporary agencies focus on providing fill-in help to their clients in all kinds of specialties without providing very much project management. Solution developers focus primarily on software development and offer documentation services as a supplemental part of a "turn-key" solution. However, some large consulting firms manage their own separate divisions that specialize in documentation and instructional design. There are a small minority of "documentation only" consulting firms that focus exclusively on technical publications and instructional design. Both temporary agencies and large consulting firms rely on a pool of permanent employees and subcontractors to deliver their service.

Figure 4-1 (continued)

Our competitive strengths

Our strengths include our technical expertise, our communication skills, and our low overhead. Our technical expertise serves the company in two ways. First, it lets us present ourselves as more technically proficient than the average technical writer. With a background in the computer industry, we can communicate more easily with software developers. Second, our technical background provides us the skills to develop the proprietary automation tools that help us to complete client projects.

Our professional communication skills reinforce our ability to not only understand the technology, but communicate it to a wide audience from novice to expert. This is an advantage when competing against a non-professional technical writer (such as a programmer or engineer) doing technical writing on the side and relying solely on their ability to understand technology.

Our low overhead is a strength when competing with large consulting firms because we can offer price advantages that these organizations cannot because they must cover the cost of sales offices and personnel.

Our competitive weaknesses

Our primary weakness is lack of resources. Current staff must provide both marketing and delivery of services. We can only take on so many projects at one time before we are maxed out. We cannot take on a very large project without subcontracting portions.

Marketing Plan

TWrite has a limited marketing budget, so we depend heavily on networking and word-of-mouth to attract new business. We will continue to pursue a strategy of including information about the business in various directories and resource guides, usually as a result of membership in relevant professional organizations. Past experience demonstrates that this is the best way to get business in this market. We do intend to increase the amount of telephone marketing, direct mail, and limited advertising to raise awareness outside of our professional circles. We don't expect to engage in active publicity such as mailing out press releases. However, the principals do intend to design seminars and write articles to raise the company's public profile.

Professional Assets

George Conrad is founder and President of TWrite, Inc. The Society for Technical Communication (STC) awarded his work in the field of technical communication.

In addition to his experience designing technical documentation, George has many years of experience in the computer industry. Before forming TWrite, he was a systems consultant for GTE Telenet and a programmer-analyst for R. R. Donnelley & Sons Company.

Figure 4-1 (continued)

Setting Your Rate Structure

The issue of setting rates sparks much controversy among independent consultants. Business experts and experienced consultants propose many methods of calculating rates. Independent consultants often argue amongst themselves about the proper time to raise or lower your going rate. Some consultants believe you should charge one rate all the time and never lower it. Others believe you should have special discounted rates for your preferred clients and a higher rate for new clients. Some believe you should never use fixed bid pricing while many swear you make the most money that way.

The most interesting aspect of these controversies is the fact that so many of them are "either-or" arguments. The fact is, to remain flexible and able to respond to market conditions, you will probably use a combination of these techniques. The trick is knowing when and where to use the right pricing technique. Most experts on calculating rates focus on calculating one fixed rate for your clients. However, if agencies are doing business in your field and you plan to work with a combination of agencies and direct clients, you will most likely maintain at least two rates—one for your direct clients and a discounted or wholesale rate for agencies. This chapter provides a strategy for creating a multilevel rate structure.

It also discusses methods for calculating rates, using fixed bids, and adjusting your rate at the proper time.

Categories of rates

The economic conditions that create a market for consulting services and the forces of supply and demand that determine a rate most clients are willing to pay are complicated. Unfortunately, there is no standard index like the Dow Jones Industrial Average for consultants. So, when trying to determine your own rate structure, on what do you base it?

For the purpose of strategizing your rate structure, I've identified common rate categories. The rate you charge at any time will probably fall into one of these categories. The purpose of these categories is to provide a method of pricing your services somewhere between a rate in which you only "break even" and the maximum rate the market will bear.

The agency rate

The agency rate is what most agencies charge their clients for your kind of work. Since agencies have full-time marketing people they have a pretty good idea what the market is for people with the skills they are selling. So, knowing what most successful agencies charge their clients gives you a pretty good picture of the top end of the market.

There are two ways to arrive at the rate an agency charges its clients. The first method is simply to ask an agency client. If you have a friend or colleague who hires agencies to do work in his or her department, you can ask what the agencies are charging for your kind of work.

The second method is to find out what agencies typically pay their subcontractors in your area and then calculate their client rate by applying an agency markup. To get an idea what agencies are willing to pay subcontractors, you can talk to other consultants and/or call up a group of agencies and ask them what rate they are willing to pay a subcontractor providing your services. That's the easy part. The hard part is finding out what number to use for the markup.

Since markup information is sensitive to each agency's business, it's hard to collect statistics that could provide a rule-of-thumb average markup rate. We can only infer an average markup from anecdotal information. To complicate matters further, there are two ways to calculate a markup. You can calculate markup as a percentage of the rate the agency *pays* the *subcontractor* or as a percentage of the rate *charged* to the *client*.

Information on the first method of calculating an agency markup is available in an article published by *Contract Professional* magazine in the July/August 1998 issue. In that article estimates by agency experts ranged from 30 to 60 percent over what they pay subcontractors. Using that range, the median value for an agency markup based on the subcontractor rate is 45 percent. For example, using the 45 percent number, and assuming you found out from your research that most agencies in your area are paying subcontractors like you $50 per hour for the same kind of work, you can roughly estimate that they charge their clients $67.50 by using the following calculation:

$$(\$50 * 0.45) + \$50 = \$67.50$$

The second method of finding a markup based on the rate charged to the client is somewhat easier to calculate. To determine a going rate equal to the rate an agency charges its clients, you might want to use the information technology industry as a model. Computer consultant expert Janet Ruhl maintains a website at www.realrates.com that conducts and maintains surveys on consultant rates and agency markups. As of this writing, her website reported the results of a survey where the median agency's markup is 38 percent. Using this number, you could arrive at an agency rate by dividing the rate an agency is willing to pay its subcontractors by 0.62. For example, if you find out that agencies are willing to pay you $50 per hour, the agency rate is calculated as about $80 per hour using the following formula:

$$\$50 / 0.62 = \$80.65$$

By now you've noticed that each method of calculating a markup arrives at a different value even when you use the same rate for what the agency is willing to pay its subcontractors. As I implied earlier, this isn't an exact science. The method you use depends on the accuracy of the information available for your business in your area. If you get more accurate information based on a markup over the subcontractor rate, use that method. If your information more accurately reflects a markup based on the rate agencies charge their clients, plug in those numbers and use that method.

The direct client rate

Your direct client rate is the rate you charge clients who come to you through your own marketing efforts. You may further divide your direct client rate into different rates depending on the type of work performed. For example, you may charge more for design or expert consulting work than for skills contracting work.

You can use the agency rate as a guide to setting your direct client rate. However, to be competitive with the agency's greater marketing resources, you may want your rates to come in at least 5 to 15 percent less than the average agency rate. Besides, clients may expect you to charge less than the larger agencies because of your lower overhead.

The wholesale rate

The wholesale rate is the rate you charge the agencies to subcontract work to you. It can also be the basis of a discount rate you charge your direct clients under certain circumstances. In either case, this should be your minimum rate. It represents the minimum profit you want to make on your work.

When dealing with agencies, you typically will not get the same rate as your direct client rate from agencies. If you do, it may be a signal you're not charging your direct clients enough! As mentioned earlier, most agencies markup their subcontractor fees, so if you quote an agency your direct client rate and they accept it without argument, it may be time to raise your direct client rate.

The break even rate

I define the break even rate for an independent consultant as the salary you would earn doing similar work as an employee plus the cost of your business expenses. While you may settle for equaling your employed salary in your first year of operation, your goal should be to make a profit in your business. If you work only to equal the salary you earned as a captive employee you are not properly compensating yourself for the added risk of running a business.

Estimating your field's going rate

Before you calculate how your rate fits into your field's rate structure, you should research the going rate for independent consultants in your field. You can use this information to compare the going rate to your minimum profitable rate to see if you're pricing yourself properly. Since the cost of living varies with location, it's important that you get rate information appropriate for your region. Some sources of rate information follow:

Industry rate surveys. Usually, the best sources of rate information are surveys published by industry organizations. Many professional organizations conduct and publish rate surveys for their members. As with any statistical surveys, the larger the sample, the better the survey. The best of these surveys include rates for both direct and agency work.

Hiring managers. If you have a friend or colleague who heads a department that routinely uses agencies and/or independent consultants, ask what rates these vendors quoted them in the past.

Networking. Attend professional meetings frequented by hiring companies or other consultants, then bring up the subject of rates among a group of other professionals. Some organizations host specific meetings whose subject is industry rates and/or salaries. You have to be careful how you address the subject, especially with other consultants, since many don't want to reveal what they charge to a potential competitor. However, you can approach the subject by referring to a recent rate survey or asking what range of rates people are seeing in the local market.

Online. Investigate online forums, chat rooms, or Internet newsgroups created for consultants in your business. Watch for discussions about rates or post questions soliciting feedback on rates for your field. Remember rates vary with locality, so make sure the rate information you get is appropriate for your region.

Government statistics. The Bureau of Labor Statistics conducts surveys on the pay of employees placed by the nation's temporary help services firms. Because these numbers are averaged, they tend to be extremely low. However, you can use them as a comparative tool to see how your field measures against others or, in conjunction with other sources of rate information, to see how your region compares with the national average for subcontracted agency work.

Calculating your rate

After you research your field's going rate, you need to calculate what I call your "profitable rate," then compare it to the going rate. There are many formulas you can use to calculate your rate; however, the best method is one that factors three basic parameters for a rate: labor, overhead, and profit.

Labor is the cost of paying yourself a reasonable salary. You can base this on the salary you were earning as an employee. However, perhaps the very reason you are considering independent consulting is because you feel you are underpaid. In this case, you may want to base your labor cost on published average salaries for your profession in your area.

Overhead is the continuing cost of running your business regardless of how much work you get. These include any costs not related to a particular client project such as rent, insurance, telephone, supplies, employment taxes, and personal benefits (health insurance, disability insurance, retirement funding, and so forth). Include any costs directly associated with a particular client project in the estimates for that project and pay for those costs from the income generated by that project. For example, if you subcontracted part of a project to another independent consultant, you would not consider the fee you pay the subcontractor as part of your business overhead (although it is part of the project's overhead).

Profit is what you earn over and above your labor and overhead costs. You may ask yourself why it is even necessary to calculate a profit. After all, your business is already compensating you for your labor. However, you would earn your labor rate whether you work for yourself or someone else. When you become an independent consultant you give up the relative safety of a regular paycheck for the risk and rewards of running your own business. Unlike a captive job, you risk your time and money in the form of overhead without any guarantee you will make one dime. Profit is your compensation for taking on that added risk. Another practical reason to calculate your profit is that you may want to plow some or all your profit back into your business by spending on equipment, marketing, training, conferences, and so forth. Using these parameters, the basic formula to calculate a profitable rate is:

Profitable rate = labor rate + overhead rate + profit

The following table provides an example of how to calculate a profitable rate. It's based on an article by Christopher Juillet included in his publication *The Meter Is Running and Other Essays*

Assumptions		Rates	
Days in year*	180	Daily labor rate (salary/days in year)	233
Salary	$42,000	Daily overhead rate (total overhead/days in year)	102
Profit margin	20%	Daily profit (daily labor rate + daily overhead rate) * profit margin	67
Overhead: Expenses and benefits	$12,000	Daily billing rate (daily labor rate + daily overhead rate + daily profit)	402
Retirement (15%)	$8,300	Hourly rate (daily billing rate/hours in day)	$50
Total overhead	$18,300		
Hours in day:	8	Gross yearly revenue (days in year * hours in day) * hourly rate	$72,360
Hours in year:	1,440	Profit (gross yearly revenue − salary − overhead)	$12,060

* 365 days − 104 weekend days − 8 holidays − 10 vacation days − 5 sick days − 58 miscellaneous days for administration, marketing, and down time = 180 days

Table 5-1: Sample calculation of a profitable rate

on Consulting. It takes into account your expenses and arrives at an hourly rate by first calculating a daily billing rate. It provides an example of this method using a salary of $42,000 and overhead expenses of $18,300.

Creating your rate strategy

After you calculate your profitable rate, you can use it to create a rate strategy that includes your direct and wholesale rates. A sample follows below.

Estimated agency rate. Assuming the minimum profitable rate matches the rate most agencies are willing to pay for these services, the estimated agency rate in this scenario is $77.

Direct rate. Our direct rate should fall between the estimated agency rate and the wholesale rate. To be competitive with the estimated agency rate, we'll calculate our direct rate as 10 percent lower than the agency rate. This gives us a direct rate of around $69 per hour.

Wholesale rate. In this scenario, we'll assume that $50 is our minimum profitable rate and serves as our discount or wholesale rate. This will be the minimum rate we charge agencies for our services.

When to consider raising your rate

As with any business, independent consulting rates respond to market conditions or to changes within your practice. When conditions change significantly enough, a rate increase may be in order. Here are some examples of situations in which you might consider raising your rates either across the board or in specific circumstances.

Increased cost of doing business. If either your labor rate or overhead costs increase and you want to maintain your profit margin, you need to raise your rates. Remember to review the salary you pay yourself the same as any manager would periodically review an employee's salary. If you discover the average salary for your industry increased, it may be time to give yourself a raise. You'll also have to increase your rates if you routinely subcontract your labor and the cost of that labor increases.

Increased demand. If you're consistently booked and you find you're turning away additional requests for your services, it indicates that demand for your services has reached a critical peak. As with any business, increased demand is typically followed by increased prices.

Increased value. You can justify an increase in rates if you've added to your skills through experience, professional development,

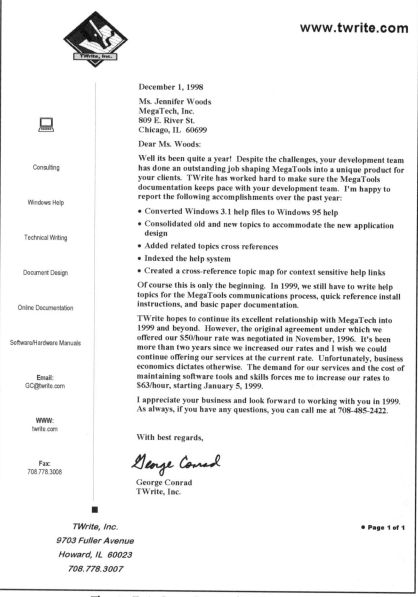

www.twrite.com

Consulting

Windows Help

Technical Writing

Document Design

Online Documentation

Software/Hardware Manuals

Email:
GC@twrite.com

WWW:
twrite.com

Fax:
708.778.3008

TWrite, Inc.
9703 Fuller Avenue
Howard, IL 60023
708.778.3007

December 1, 1998

Ms. Jennifer Woods
MegaTech, Inc.
809 E. River St.
Chicago, IL 60699

Dear Ms. Woods:

Well its been quite a year! Despite the challenges, your development team has done an outstanding job shaping MegaTools into a unique product for your clients. TWrite has worked hard to make sure the MegaTools documentation keeps pace with your development team. I'm happy to report the following accomplishments over the past year:

• Converted Windows 3.1 help files to Windows 95 help
• Consolidated old and new topics to accommodate the new application design
• Added related topics cross references
• Indexed the help system
• Created a cross-reference topic map for context sensitive help links

Of course this is only the beginning. In 1999, we still have to write help topics for the MegaTools communications process, quick reference install instructions, and basic paper documentation.

TWrite hopes to continue its excellent relationship with MegaTech into 1999 and beyond. However, the original agreement under which we offered our $50/hour rate was negotiated in November, 1996. It's been more than two years since we increased our rates and I wish we could continue offering our services at the current rate. Unfortunately, business economics dictates otherwise. The demand for our services and the cost of maintaining software tools and skills forces me to increase our rates to $63/hour, starting January 5, 1999.

I appreciate your business and look forward to working with you in 1999. As always, if you have any questions, you can call me at 708-485-2422.

With best regards,

George Conrad

George Conrad
TWrite, Inc.

● Page 1 of 1

Figure 5-1: Sample rate increase letter

and/or new services. You also increase your value if your industry recognizes you by distinguishing your work with industry awards.

Rising industry rates. If you find other consultants with the same or lesser skills are successfully charging more for their work, it may indicate that the going rate for your field is rising and you should raise yours accordingly.

Stagnant rate. You should review your rates at least every two years. As a general rule, if you haven't raised your rates in two years, it's probably time to consider an increase.

How do you inform your current clients about a rate increase? I suggest you send a rate increase letter outlining accomplishments achieved while working with the client. Then explain your rate increase. If you value the client, try to offer some money-saving options such as volume discounts for blocks of consulting hours.

When to consider charging less

Besides the fact that you will discount your rate for agencies, you will encounter other situations when you will consider temporarily reducing your rates. Here are some basic situations in which you should consider reducing your rate.

Target new clients. New clients may hesitate to try a new consultant, so to get the business you could offer a "new client discount" rate on the first project. Another way you can target new clients is to publish coupons in trade papers offering several initial hours of consulting for free. Make sure the client understands this is a "one-time only" offer and that your standard rate will kick in at some point.

Stimulate business during a slow cycle. Your industry may experience seasonal cycles of feast and famine. During slow periods you may want to offer a "seasonal discount" in which you offer a discount to new and existing clients for a specified period of time. To alert your current clients, you could send them an announcement about your special seasonal rate.

Reward a loyal client. You may want to offer a special discount or your wholesale rate to a client with whom you have a special relationship. There are several reasons why you might want to do this. Perhaps the client has consistently patronized your business for a long time and you want to keep them happy. Maybe the client has a project that you find particularly appealing even though they can't budget for your full rate.

Regulate cash flow. To encourage clients to hire you for longer periods of time, you may want to offer a "volume discount" in which you discount your rate if the client commits to a minimum number of hours. You can also offer a discount if the client pre-pays hours or hires you on a "retainer" basis. This is a win-win situation because you get your money up front and the client gets a discount or at least protection from a price increase.

Methods of payment

Getting paid on an hourly basis is only one of several payment methods. You may use more than one of these methods depending on the client situation and the type of work. Here are the more common payment methods along with their advantages and disadvantages.

Hourly. This is the method used by most consultants. The advantage is you get compensated for every hour you spend on the project. The disadvantage is you receive no reward for completing a project early. When you get paid on an hourly basis, you have to decide how the client will compensate you for project expenses beyond your project hours. For example, it may make sense to bill the client separately for items such as duplication, overnight mail, or production materials.

Fixed bid. When you bid for a project based on a *fixed bid*, the client pays you one price for the entire project regardless of how long it takes you to complete. Consultants also refer to this as a "project fee." A typical scenario is to request one-third payment up front, one-third when a project milestone is reached, and final payment when you complete the project. The advantage to this method is that if you work efficiently and complete the project according to your estimate or even ahead of schedule you could make a larger profit than the same time paid hourly. The disadvantage is that if you do not meet your estimate you could end up working for a fraction of your hourly rate.

Fixed bid projects work best when you control the design and delivery of the solution. For example, a standard repetitive procedure like conducting a survey you designed yourself would be appropriate for fixed bid projects. But be wary of projects that depend on constantly changing technology. In these cases, technical writing consultant Candace Masella prefers to give a project *estimate* with a built in reassessment period. "Halfway through the project we evaluate the project's status and let the client know if we expect to exceed the estimate to complete the project as outlined in the project requirements section of our proposal. If they approve, we proceed with the rest of the project. If they do not, we let them know exactly what we can accomplish based on the remaining funds."

Day rate. Besides charging by the hour, you can charge by the day. The advantage is, similar to an hourly rate, you get paid incrementally. The disadvantage is a client may define a "day" differently than you. The client may expect you to do ten- or twelve-hour days. This method works best for projects that are easily broken into day increments such as training classes.

Prepaid. Prepaid agreements typically offer a discount for purchasing a fixed number of hours before the hours are actually delivered. The advantage is you get your money from the client ahead of time. The disadvantage is that if you do not define an expiration time limit for delivering the hours, the client could drag out the unused hours forever, messing up your scheduling for other projects.

Retainer. Under a retainer agreement, you bill the client a fixed-fee regularly in exchange for being available to the client on an as-needed basis. This is common in the legal, public relations, and advertising fields. In the technology industry, this usually takes the form of a service agreement. The advantage is you get a consistent cash flow. The disadvantage is that if you do not carefully define the parameters of the retainer, you could be "on the hook" to the client for more work than the retainer justifies. Also, you have to be flexible enough to respond to the client when they request your time. As with the prepaid method, you should carefully define how much time is included in the retainer and the disposition of unused hours.

The Legal Form of Your Business and Tax Issues

"It was as true as taxes is. And nothing's truer than them."

—Charles Dickens (1812–1870), English novelist
Mr. Barkis in *David Copperfield* (1849–1850)

This chapter provides an overview of various types of business entities. It is not intended to substitute or replace the advice of an attorney, accountant, or other similar professional. Before making any critical decisions regarding the setup of your business, you should consult the appropriate licensed professional.

There are five basic legal forms your business can take: sole proprietor, partnership, S corporation, C corporation, and Limited Liability Corporation (LLC). Of these, I will not discuss LLCs because few independent consultants use this form of business and not every state allows them.

This chapter includes discussion of temporary employee status as a contractor, which is not technically a form of business. For many independent consultants, however, this is the first type of contractual relationship they enter into, so you should be aware of its advantages and limitations.

The types of business structures available to you are shaped by two basic factors: liability and taxation. A sole proprietor and partnership assumes more personal liability risk than a corporation. This means that the chances of a lawsuit awarding damages against the personal assets of a sole proprietor or partner is greater than that of a shareholder of a corporation. Taxation is a fact of life for any type of business. Depending on the type of business, the IRS charges taxes against the business owner's personal income or against the profits of the business. Contract employees, sole proprietors, partnerships, and S corporations pay taxes based on the owner's net income from the business. C corporations pay separate taxes based on the net profits of the business. Each business type has various liability and taxation advantages and disadvantages.

When considering which legal form you will ultimately choose for your business entity—you should consider how the business pays you, how the IRS gets paid, and the effort required to set up the business.

Except in a contract employee arrangement, you must justify the IRS definition of an independent contractor when you work for either a client or an agency, regardless of the legal form of business you choose. If you fail to meet the IRS definition of an independent contractor, the IRS could make your client or agency liable for payroll taxes and disallow your business deductions.

Contract employee arrangement

When someone hires you as a contract employee, you are not a business but a temporary employee. This is typically the type of relationship you establish when you first start working with agencies. Per your contract, your employer issues you a paycheck which includes your net pay, after taxes, for the pay period.

The IRS gets paid when your employer withholds federal, state, social security, Medicare, and any other taxes typical for employees in your area. You fill out a W-4 and receive a W-2 same as any other employee. The IRS tracks you for tax purposes using your Social Security number entered on the W-4 form.

The only paperwork necessary to set up a contract employee is to fill out a W-4 form for your employer. This registers your Social Security number and establishes the number of allowances you want to set for withholding purposes.

This is the easiest method of employment to set up. As a temporary employee, you may qualify to participate in some employer benefits such as health insurance and retirement plans. However, you usually have to work for the employer for a minimum number of hours per year before you qualify.

Although your employer withholds payroll taxes from your paycheck, you avoid paying the employer side of Social Security and Medicare taxes. As of this writing, these taxes add up to 7.65 percent of your gross earnings. This includes 6.2 percent of Social Security tax on the first $68,400 of gross earnings and 1.45 percent of Medicare tax on all your earnings. You also avoid paying federal and state unemployment taxes.

Another advantage is limited liability. As a contract employee, you are shielded from liability against the hiring company when you act as an agent for that company.

Disadvantages include the fact you cannot deduct business expenses while you are a temporary employee. This means you typically cannot deduct the cost of your home office, equipment, or any of your health insurance costs. However, there are some exceptions to this restriction. If you file itemized deductions for personal deductible expenses (mortgage payments, real estate taxes, and so forth), you can also deduct the expenses of nonreimbursed items, such as equipment or uniforms, required by your employer.

Sole proprietor status

If you do not work for someone as a temporary employee and you do not set up a corporation or partnership, your business legally defaults to a sole proprietorship. After you do work for a client as a sole proprietor, the client issues you and the IRS a 1099 statement describing how much the client paid you during the year.

You get paid by withdrawing as little or as much as you want from the profits of your business. The IRS gets paid when you report the net profit of your business on your personal income taxes using Schedule C. You must file a declaration of estimated income tax (Form 1040-ES) each quarter. When you file Form 1040-ES you pay estimated federal income taxes and self-employment taxes for the quarter. The self-employment tax includes both the employer and employee portions of the Social

Security and Medicare taxes totaling 15.3 percent. If you do not have employees, the IRS tracks the business for tax purposes using your personal Social Security number. If you hire employees, you must file for a Federal Employer ID number using form SS-4.

Although you do not have to fill out any paperwork to establish a sole proprietorship, you may need to register with your local government. This may include filing a fictitious name statement or Doing Business As (DBA) name. You may also have to apply for a local business license from your county or municipality.

An advantage to a sole proprietorship is you can deduct your business expenses including at least a portion of your health insurance costs. You apply the deduction to your adjusted gross income, not to the Schedule C for your business.

A disadvantage is a sole proprietorship does not protect your personal assets from damages assessed as the result of a lawsuit against your business.

Partnerships

Although partnerships are typical for law firms and architectural firms, partnerships are rare for most other independent consultants. A partnership is the only form of business that *requires* multiple owners. Even a corporation can be owned by only one person. As an alternative to a partnership, most consultants create a corporation and distribute shares to other owners when they want to add people to their business.

The way you get paid is determined by a partnership agreement. Typically, the agreement divides profits equally between the partners.

The IRS gets paid by taxing the profits of the individual partners. The IRS requires partnerships to file a partnership income tax return (Form 1065) even though the partnership itself does not pay any taxes. Form 1065 includes an attached form K-1 that shows the changes in each partner's share and the taxable share of the partnership's income or loss. A partnership must also obtain a Federal Employer ID number even if it has no employees.

Other than the IRS forms mentioned above, the government does not require any formal paperwork to set up a partnership.

However, though it is not required by law, most partnerships create a written partnership agreement, usually drawn up by an attorney.

One advantage to a partnership is it relieves you from doing everything yourself. If you allocate the work load properly, you can have one partner do marketing full-time while another delivers the service.

Similar to a sole proprietorship, a partnership is legally connected to its owners. This means that a court can order the partners to pay the damages of a lawsuit from the partners' personal assets.

S corporations

S corporation refers to Subchapter S of the Internal Revenue Code. An S corporation is a cross between a standard corporation and a partnership. It's like a corporation because ownership is vested in shareholders and it provides limited liability protection to the company stockholders. It's like a partnership because it provides for multiple owners and all the profits of the S corporation pass through to the shareholders where the IRS taxes the profits as personal income.

There are two ways to receive money from your S corporation. You can pay yourself as an employee of your corporation complete with payroll deductions and W-2 form at the end of the year. The second method is to withdraw profits in the form of a distribution. The primary advantage of paying yourself a salary (despite the cost of payroll deductions) is that it qualifies you for your company retirement plan and you continue to participate in the federal Social Security program. When you pay yourself a distribution, the IRS taxes it as part of your total income on your personal income taxes. You avoid payroll taxes, but none of the money from the distribution can participate in a retirement program.

As you pay yourself a salary, you withhold taxes from your paycheck the same as any other employer would. When you deposit the withheld funds, you must add the 7.65 percent employer side taxes for Social Security and Medicare. The S corporation must file an income tax return (Form 1120-S). Any taxable income the business earns (in excess of your salary and expenses) pass through to you on your personal income taxes using Schedule E.

Each individual state, not the federal government, registers and licenses corporations. No two corporations can have the same name within the same state, so you have to reserve your corporate name then file articles of incorporation and pay a licensing fee. Usually the articles of incorporation is a standard form that you fill out. Every year you file an annual report and pay a yearly franchise tax.

The S corporation designation is an IRS issue and as such is not handled by the states. To register your corporation as an S corporation, you have to file Form 2553 with the IRS prior to the taxable year for which it will be effective, or by the fifteenth day of the third month of the current taxable year. Also, you must get a Federal Employer Tax ID number from the IRS (Form SS-4). Finally, you must set up a corporate checking account separate from your personal checking account.

The most often-sited advantage to incorporating (S or C corporation) is the limited liability. If a lawsuit can show that you incorporated for the sole purpose of avoiding liability while acting recklessly, or if you don't maintain your corporate status (such as neglecting to file your annual report and paying the franchise tax), the lawsuit may expose your personal assets. This is known as "piercing the corporate veil." Despite this possibility, incorporating does provide an additional hurdle for someone seeking damages beyond the assets of the corporation itself.

Many independent consultants incorporate to add prestige to their business and to access more clients. Having "Inc." or "Corp." after the name of your company reinforces that yours is a "serious" business.

An added advantage of S corporations is in the area of taxes. S corporations do not pay corporation taxes like standard corporations. If your S corporation sustains a loss in the first year of operation, the losses can "fall through" to you offsetting your personal tax burden.

In general, the biggest disadvantage to incorporating is increased paperwork and cost. As noted previously, you have to file annual reports with the state and a corporate tax return with the IRS. Additionally, you have to handle all the employer paperwork to pay yourself a salary.

S corporations also have many specialized restrictions. S corporations are limited to 75 or fewer stockholders and must use the same tax year as their shareholders, which is January 1 through December 31. More significant, however, are the restrictions on deductions. An S corporation cannot deduct the cost of any employee fringe benefits (health, accident, life, disability insurance, and so forth) for any employees who own 2 percent or more of the company's stock. This excludes most independent consultants who typically own 100 percent of their company's stock.

C corporations

When you incorporate, if you don't register as an S corporation, the IRS automatically classifies your corporation as a C corporation. The primary difference between S and C type corporations is that C corporations pay corporate income taxes on any profits leftover after salaries and other expenses. If you want to receive a dividend in addition to your salary from the C corporation, you receive income that the IRS already taxed at the corporate level. You must report that dividend as income on your personal taxes where the IRS taxes you again. This double taxation encourages most independent consultants to start with S corporations and then convert to C corporations when they want to take advantage of the added deductions.

Technically, as with S corporations, there are two ways to receive money from your C corporation. You can pay yourself as an employee of your corporation and/or you can pay yourself a distribution in the form of a dividend. As explained previously, if you pay out dividends, you get double-taxed. The advantage of paying yourself a salary is that it qualifies you for any corporate employee benefits based on your salary, including retirement saving benefits.

You handle any employee salaries the same as an S corporation or any company that pays employees on a W-2 basis. The IRS taxes any profits the business earns (in excess of your salary and expenses) at the corporate tax rate. C corporations must also deposit estimated income taxes every quarter.

As discussed above for S corporations, the states register and license corporations. All the standard corporate advantages sited above for S corporations also apply to C corporations including limited liability, increased prestige, and access to more clients. The biggest additional advantage that C corporations have is the ability to deduct the cost of any employee fringe benefits. This includes items such as health, accident, life, and disability insurance, regardless of the level of employee ownership. Also, C corporations can select what constitutes their tax year. This could provide some advantages when trying to balance the interplay between corporate and shareholder cash flow and taxes.

The biggest disadvantage of C corporations is the double taxation. Also, there's additional paperwork in the form of quarterly estimated taxes.

Are you an employee?

As an independent consultant, sooner or later you will encounter clients hesitant to hire you for fear the IRS may reclassify you as their employee. If you are reclassified as an employee of one of your clients, they may have to pay IRS penalties and include you in their employee benefits package. If this happens, the primary risk to you is that the IRS disallows your business deductions. This situation is actually rather rare, but several high-profile cases have caused company managers to pause before hiring independent consultants. Some companies even have standing policies not to hire any contractors unless they work for agencies with five or more employees. It is to your advantage to understand how the IRS defines employees and independent contractors.

The IRS "20 factors"

The guiding factor the IRS uses to determine if you are an employee or independent contractor is the famous "20 factors" or "20 questions." The 20 factors expands a common-law test meant to establish who has *control* of your work. In a nutshell, if the person who employs you sets your work hours, provides you with tools, tells you what to do and how to do it, and can fire you, then the IRS is inclined to consider you an employee. It doesn't matter if the employer allows you freedom of action in your work. Just the fact that the employer has the legal right to control the result and method of your work is enough to demonstrate an employer-employee relationship.

What makes the application of the 20 factors so difficult is that the IRS does not consistently apply all the factors. In certain circumstances, you could technically answer more than half the questions as an employee, but still be an independent contractor because of the way the IRS weighs the questions for a particular situation. Check the IRS Web site at http://irs.ustreas.gov for the latest information on the IRS 20 factors.

Safe harbor

Over the past couple of decades, the IRS has steadily increased its enforcement of the employment tax laws with regard to employee classification. However, the 20 factors used by the IRS raised some problems. One of the stronger indications of client control is the necessity for an independent contractor to work at the client's premises. There are, however, many situations where legitimate independent contractors have to work at the client's premises because that's where the object of the work is located. A lawn care company *must* work on its client's premises because that's where the lawn is located. Likewise, the government could hardly expect mainframe programmer consultants to purchase a mainframe just so they can complete client work on their own premises.

Because of these vagaries and the increased attention brought by the IRS, the government enacted Section 530 of the 1978 Tax Reform Act to include what is now called a Safe Harbor clause. This legislation was originally intended as a temporary relief measure and was scheduled to terminate at the end of 1979, but instead, congress decided to extend it indefinitely. The clause exempted certain workers from having to meet all 20 factors to qualify as independent contractors. It allowed a client to treat an individual as a contractor, regardless of the 20 factors, if the client consistently treated the worker and similar workers as independent contractors, filed all required forms such as 1099s, *and* had a reasonable basis for treating the worker as an independent contractor. This includes similar rulings or court cases that upheld the independent contractor status, longstanding industry-wide practice, or failure of prior IRS tax auditors to question the status of the independent contractors.

Section 1706

If you plan to do consulting in what the IRS considers the "technical service" sector and you will be working through agencies, you should know about Section 1706. Section 1706(a) of the 1986 Tax Reform Act added a new subsection (d) to Section 530 of the 1978 Act. Even though you have to look in Section 530(d) to find the code, most people refer to Section 1706 when discussing this issue.

Section 1706 removes the Safe Harbor protection for agencies that hire independent contractors in the technical services industry. The section is poorly written and was so confusing that the IRS issued a clarification which confirmed that the new law would apply only to three-party relationships between an agency, contractor, and client. The *actual wording* of the section is as follows: "Section 530 shall not apply in the case of an individual who, pursuant to an arrangement between the taxpayer and another person, provides services for such other person as an engineer, designer, drafter, computer programmer, systems analyst, or other similarly skilled worker engaged in a similar line of work."

Huh? You can see why organizations like the Independent Computer Consultants Association (ICCA) have tried to get Congress to repeal this legislation since it was passed in 1986. Janet Ruhl, in her book *The Computer Consultant's Guide*, provides an excellent description of the history of Section 1706. Apparently, the legislation was inserted into the tax code due to lobbying efforts by the National Technical Services Association (NTSA), an organization dominated by large technical service agencies. NTSA stated that its goal was to force temporary technical workers to work as salaried employees to tip the competitive edge to the larger firms who made up its membership.

NTSA lobbied for the legislation on the basis of their competitive disadvantage against smaller agencies who could attract more skilled technical contractors because the smaller agencies were willing to treat them as independent contractors and as a result share with them a much larger part of the client billings. In addition to NTSA's lobbying, IRS studies at the time *seemed* to indicate independent contractors were more likely to under report income and claim unwarranted deductions. Based on these factors, Congress decided to restrict Section 1706 to technical service workers, and the legislation was quietly slipped into the larger Tax Reform Act of 1986 without any public debate.

If you are a technical services independent consultant, you face two basic problems related to Section 1706. The first is that because of the confusing wording of the section, some direct clients think they do not qualify for the Safe Harbor clause when they hire you directly as an independent consultant. In this case, you can try to educate your client as to the real application of the section in three-party arrangements. This is also a good reason to incorporate, because many clients who are worried about Section 1706 feel more protected when you are incorporated.

The second problem you face occurs when you do work through an agency. In this situation, incorporation by itself does not protect the agency from Section 1706, although many believe it does. When doing work through an agency, as much as possible, you should try to reinforce your status as an independent consultant as defined in the IRS 20 factors. Some agencies don't want to risk being burned, so they only hire consultants as temporary employees on a W-2 basis. If you encounter an agency with this policy, you could take the W-2 work; however, you should be aware that if you mix W-2 and independent consultant work the IRS could redefine all your work as W-2. The simplest way to avoid this is to turn down any work that requires you to work on a W-2 basis.

Insurance

> *"Insurance. An ingenious modern game of chance in which the player is permitted to enjoy the comfortable conviction that he is beating the man who keeps the table."*
>
> —Ambrose Bierce (1842–1914), U.S. author
> *The Devil's Dictionary* (1881–1906)

Most people avoid the subject of insurance like the plague. As consumers, we are used to dealing with homeowners, auto, and life insurance. As employees, we take for granted insurance that our employers provide such as disability, health, and business liability.

Although many self-employed business owners recognize the need for health insurance, they tend to skimp on other essential protection. If you think you can save money by cutting out disability or business liability insurance, read this chapter. With competition in the insurance industry, the cost of having the right kind of insurance for your business far outweighs the cost of taking a risk. You don't have to get every expensive insurance option, but without minimal protection, your business is only one catastrophe away from disaster.

Personal benefits insurance

Some clients are surprised to see what independent consultants charge per hour for their work when they compare the consultant's rate to their own salary. What they do not realize is that unlike them, you have to pay for your own personal benefits package. A large portion of this package consists of items that salaried employees often take for granted: health, disability, and life insurance.

Health insurance

Traditionally, self-employed people experience difficulty purchasing health insurance. As an independent consultant, you probably never get the economies of scale that a large company does when it purchases health insurance for its employees. Options for independent consultants seeking health insurance have improved over the last few years as some commercial insurers and HMOs start to provide more products designed for the self-employed. Some common sources of health insurance for independent consultants include the following.

COBRA. If you recently left a job with a company that employed 20 or more workers, you qualify for coverage under COBRA. COBRA stands for Consolidated Omnibus Budget Reconciliation Act, which took effect on April 7, 1986. It allows you to continue under your previous company's group health insurance plan for up to 18 months after you leave the company. To use this plan, you must pay the company's premiums plus up to 2 percent for administrative expenses. However, these premiums are often less than those for an individual policy, making COBRA a good deal.

Make sure you pay the premiums on time. The industry estimates that an employee or dependent receives $2 in benefits for each $1 of premium paid under COBRA. Because of this, employers use late payment of premiums as an excuse to discontinue COBRA coverage for employees.

I suggest you use COBRA only as a temporary "filler" policy until you find a permanent health care policy. You shouldn't wait until the entire 18-month period is used up before settling on a permanent policy. "You should apply for permanent health insurance at least eight weeks before your COBRA runs out," says Mary Micheff, an American Family Insurance agent. "It usually takes six to eight weeks for the company underwriting the COBRA policy to obtain and transfer your medical records from doctors and hospitals."

Spouse's policy. If you are married and your spouse has a job that provides health insurance to the families of its employees, you and the rest of your family can be added to your spouse's policy. This is probably your least expensive option because you take advantage of your spouse's company's group rate. After assuming this responsibility in our household, my wife started calling herself the "keeper of the healthcare."

Individual policies. The most ubiquitous source of individual policies is nonprofit Blue Cross/Blue Shield. Blue Cross is available nationwide and will sell a policy to a self-employed person. However, you will pay more than an employee of a large company contracting to Blue Cross for their health insurance.

Commercial insurers. Commercial insurers typically service only larger businesses with 50 or more employees. Some do provide plans for one-person businesses.

Professional membership group policies. Many large associations and professional groups select an insurance company to provide discount or group insurance for their members. In addition to these organizations, your local chamber of commerce may offer health insurance plans to its members. When you consider these plans, make sure they are offered by stable companies.

State legislated health care plans. Some states, such as Hawaii, Vermont, Oregon, and Florida, provide "universal" health plans that offer affordable health insurance to its residents. Other states are considering similar plans. Check with your state's government agencies to see if you qualify for a state health insurance plan and compare that plan to other options available to you.

Disability insurance

Disability insurance is the most often overlooked insurance for independent consultants. It's also the one type of insurance an independent consultant is most likely to go without. It's one of those benefits that you took for granted as a captive employee, but must now provide for yourself as an independent consultant.

Disability insurance provides you an income when you are unable to work due to illness or injury. If you are disabled due to illness or injury for more than 90 days, statistically the average duration of that disability will continue for at least five years.

If you consider a 32-year-old person is 3.5 times more likely to be disabled for 90 days (or more) than die at that age, disability insurance should be near the top of your insurance requirements list. One of the advantages of purchasing your own disability insurance is that unlike an employee whose company provides this benefit paid for with pretax dollars, you pay for your disability insurance with after-tax dollars. This means you receive any benefit payments tax-free.

There are two main sources of disability policies for independent consultants: professional organizations and individual policies. Professional organizations can either provide disability insurance automatically as part of group coverage with your membership or simply refer you to their "approved" insurance provider to get an individual policy at a discount.

I suggest you do not depend on group disability policies provided by professional organizations. Although they may seem like a good deal, you have no control over a group policy that may have weak definitions of disability and could be terminated by the insurance provider. I suggest you stick with an individual policy where you deal directly with the insurance provider and you can select the level of coverage that's best for you.

Get a policy that covers you if you cannot perform your chosen occupation. Otherwise, the insurer will no longer consider you disabled if you can perform *any* kind of work. Look for a policy that cannot be canceled and is guaranteed renewable to age 65. This keeps the insurer from increasing the premiums beyond the contract provisions regardless of health problems you encounter along the way.

You should also opt for a cost-of-living adjustment. This adjusts your benefits upward, based on the Consumer Price Index (CPI), each year you continue to be disabled after the first year. You can reduce the cost of your premiums by lengthening the period of time between a disabling incident and when you start receiving payments. This is known as an "elimination" or "waiting" period. Typically, the most cost-effective period is 90 days, provided you have sufficient financial resources to cover your expenses until you receive your first payment. You can also reduce your premiums by shortening the period of time during which the insurer pays you benefits. You can select a payout period ranging from one year to life. The most common time periods are two years, five years, and to age 65.

Life insurance

How much, if any, life insurance you purchase depends largely on your family situation. To decide how much life insurance you need, you must ask yourself, "If I die, who will experience economic hardship?" If you are single with no dependents, perhaps the answer is "no one" and you may decide to skip life insurance entirely, at least for now. If you are the sole wage earner for a family of four, you should consider some coverage.

A full discussion of the different types of life insurance is beyond the scope of this book. All life insurance polices do have some things in common. The price of all life insurance policies is based on two common costs: mortality and expenses. The insurance company calculates *mortality* charges to cover the amount the policy promises to pay if you die. The policy incurs *expense* charges from issuing and managing the policy.

There are two basic types of life insurance: term and whole life. With *term* insurance, you pay only for the mortality and expense charges (and no more) for the term of the policy (usually one year). At the end of the term, there is no investment value to the policy. With *whole life*, you pay more than the cost of basic mortality and expense charges. When you pay more in your premium than is required for the current year's mortality and expense charges, the insurance company invests the difference in the form of a dividend, in an investment account attached to the policy. The investment vehicle can be stocks, mutual funds, annuities, and so forth.

Some people feel that the investment vehicles offered by insurance policies don't make good investments. When they need life insurance, they purchase renewable term insurance and invest the difference themselves. One advantage of whole life is that the government does not tax dividends paid on life insurance provided they do not exceed the total premiums paid into the policy. Also, as agent Mary Micheff points out, "Life insurance benefits paid to the beneficiary are tax free, provided you, the insured, not the business, are paying the premiums."

Regardless of the type of insurance you decide to purchase, I suggest you use an insurance broker rather than an agent of a particular company. Insurance brokers can reference the full range of insurance products offered by many companies to find you the best deal whereas as an agent is tied to the products of his or her particular company.

Business insurance

In addition to insuring yourself, your business requires some insurance. This includes general business liability, equipment, workers compensation, and errors and omissions.

General business liability insurance

General business liability insurance covers you or one of your employees for accidental damage someone from your company may cause on a client's property. It also covers your company for accidental injuries during events you stage, such as training seminars or luncheons. It typically *does not* cover you for professional malpractice or mistakes made in your work (see errors and omissions, below).

Some clients require their vendors carry minimal business liability insurance and ask the vendor to include them in the policy's list of additional insured persons or organizations. Once you have a general business liability insurance policy, you can add the name of your client to this list. Most insurance companies can complete this task in less than a day. Some do it for free while others charge an extra fee for this service. Since more client contracts require this insurance and it's relatively inexpensive, you should consider general business liability insurance part of your cost of doing business.

Equipment insurance

Considering the damage caused by the loss of your equipment due to theft or fire, business equipment insurance is essential. If you do work from your home, you should be aware that most homeowners insurance does not automatically cover your business equipment, so you may need to purchase separate business equipment insurance.

Even though the case for business equipment insurance is clear-cut, you still have to act responsibly to protect your business from an equipment disaster. Although an equipment insurance policy allows you to replace lost equipment and even software, no amount of insurance can replace lost client work or data files, so back it up!

Workers compensation

Workers compensation insurance compensates employees for costs of work-related injuries and time off the job. This type of insurance is regulated and standardized by state government. You will probably purchase this insurance from a broker representing an insurance pool for small businesses. Although your state may not require you to get this insurance for your business, many clients require it so they feel protected if you injure yourself while working on their premises.

You might be able to get a client to accept an appropriate health insurance policy instead of workers compensation if the policy covers you for 24 hours or during periods of work. However, it may be difficult to convince the client that this provides the same coverage as workers compensation insurance while you're working and it will only cover *you* under *your* personal health insurance. If other employees or 1099 subcontractors of your company are not under the same health insurance plan, they will not be covered. As agent Micheff points out, it could be costly if you don't cover your employees and 1099 subcontractors. "As a sole proprietor or officer of a corporation, you can exclude yourself from coverage. However, if an employee or subcontractor works for your company, you are responsible for that person's medical bills and approximately 66 percent of the person's pay if that person is injured on the job regardless if you pay them on a W-2 or 1099."

Errors and omissions

This type of insurance covers you against claims alleging financial loss arising from mistakes in the work or services you delivered to a client. Unlike general business liability insurance, it can continue to cover you for a period of years after you complete work for a client.

This type of insurance is expensive and difficult to find. Some clients ask for it in their contracts, but you can negotiate to remove this requirement rather than purchase the insurance. If you work in a high-risk industry, you may have to accept this as a cost of doing business and factor it into your rates. Some professional organizations, such as the Independent Computer Consultants Association (ICCA), offer its members errors and omissions insurance tailored to the needs of its industry.

Retirement Funding—The Hidden Benefit

8

> *"I advise you to go on living solely to enrage those who are paying your annuities. It is the only pleasure I have left."*
>
> —Voltaire (1694–1778), French philosopher, author
> letter dated April 23, 1754, to Madame du Deffand

One of the often overlooked benefits to working for yourself is that you get to decide how and where to put your retirement dollars. When you work for someone else and participate in their retirement program, your employer provides you with a limited number of preselected choices in which you can invest your retirement dollars. Often employers make these choices not because they represent the best investment options for their employees, but because the selected plan has the lowest management fees and the least amount of hassle for the employer.

Employers seldom consult employees during the retirement plan selection process. As an independent consultant with your own business, you can choose from a wide array of retirement plans including an Individual Retirement Account (IRA), Simplified Employee Pension (SEP), Keogh, or the newer Savings Incentive Match Plan for Employees (SIMPLE).

Although this chapter provides an overview of various types of retirement plans, it's not intended to substitute for the advice of an attorney, accountant, or qualified financial planner. Before you set up your retirement plan, I strongly urge you to consult the appropriate financial professional.

Individual Retirement Account (IRA)

An IRA is a personal retirement account rather than one you set up through your company. This makes an IRA the simplest type of retirement account to set up. However, Congress recently made many changes to the IRA. Currently you have the following choices:

Standard IRA (deductible)

If you are not participating in any other employer-sponsored retirement plan, you can fully contribute to a standard IRA up to $2,000 a year and deduct your contribution from your earned income. You cannot contribute more than you make in a year. For instance, if you made only $1,500 in your independent consulting business, you can only deduct a maximum of $1,500.

Essentially, you can start withdrawing funds from your IRA at age 59½ and *must* start withdrawing at age 70½. When you start withdrawing money from an IRA during retirement, the IRS considers your withdrawals as income (except for nondeductible contributions discussed below) and you start paying taxes on the money in the same way as if it was a salary. That's why people call standard IRAs tax *deferred* accounts rather than tax *free* accounts.

If you participate in another employer-sponsored retirement plan (such as one offered by an agency who subcontracted work to you on a W-2 basis), how much you make determines how much you can contribute to your own standard IRA. The thresholds for deductible contributions change from year to year and depend on whether you are single or married filling jointly.

In 1997, for instance, if you were single or head of a household and you earned less than $25,000 under another plan, you could still deduct up to $2,000 per year from your taxes for contributions to a standard IRA. If you earned between $25,000 and $35,000, the IRS prorated the deductible portion of your contribution on a declining basis. If you earned $35,000 or more under another plan, you could not deduct any of your contribution from your taxes.

If you are married, filing jointly, the IRS provides higher thresholds. In 1997, if your household income was less than $40,000 under another plan, you could still deduct contributions up to $2,000 per year. If your household income was between $40,000 and $50,000, the IRS prorated deductibility. If your household income was $50,000 or more under another plan, you could not deduct any of your contribution from your taxes.

The Taxpayer Relief Act of 1997 (TRA 97) incrementally raises the ceilings for deductibility between 1997 and 2007. In 2005, the phase-out range for single taxpayers will raise to $50,000 to $60,000. In 2007, the phase-out range for married taxpayers will raise to $80,000 to $100,000.

TRA 97 also decouples you and your spouse when only one of you participates in an employer-sponsored retirement plan. The spouse who does not participate in an employee-sponsored plan can deduct 100 percent of his or her IRA contributions (up to the $2,000 limit), provided your combined Adjusted Gross Income (AGI) does not exceed $150,000. Be sure to consult a professional financial planner and/or accountant each year to assess how changes from TRA 97 affect your situation.

Standard IRA (nondeductible)

Even if you cannot deduct any portion of contributions you made to an IRA, you can always still contribute up to $2,000 of your earned income into a standard IRA account every year regardless of your income level. It's just that you cannot deduct the contribution from your earned income. Any dividends or interest generated by the money you contribute still accumulates tax deferred until you take it out during retirement. However, the government taxes the IRA's earnings (dividends, gains, and interest) when you withdraw these funds at retirement.

If you decide to make nondeductible contributions to your standard IRA, make sure you or your accountant file the appropriate forms with your tax return every year to track the nondeductible money you contribute each year. Since you're contributing after-tax money, you'll want to file these forms so the IRS doesn't try to tax you again on this money when you withdraw it during retirement.

Roth IRA

TRA 97 also created an entirely new plan, the Roth IRA. Named after its sponsor, Senate Finance Committee Chairman William Roth, this new IRA allows you to make qualified withdrawals from your IRA free from federal taxes. The maximum ceilings to qualify for a Roth IRA are $110,000 for single taxpayers and $160,000 for joint taxpayers. If you earn between $95,000 and $110,000 for single taxpayers or between $150,000 and $160,000 for joint taxpayers, the law reduces the amount you can contribute.

If you qualify for a Roth IRA, you can make nondeductible contributions up to $2,000 per year. In this sense, the Roth IRA is similar to the standard nondeductible IRA contribution. Unlike standard nondeductible contributions, all earnings (dividends, gains, and interest) are free from federal taxes when you make a withdrawal. You can start making withdrawals at age 59½, provided it's been at least five years since your first contribution. You may still have to pay state and/or local taxes.

There are other advantages to Roth IRAs, such as the ability to withdraw funds for first-time home purchases (up to $10,000), higher education costs, and other special circumstances. You can convert a standard IRA to a Roth IRA if you are willing to pay the one-time tax conversion costs. I suggest you consult a qualified financial professional for these and other details on the Roth IRA.

Simplified Employee Pension (SEP)

A SEP IRA retirement program is a middle option between an IRA and a Keogh plan. It provides the simplicity of a personal IRA with increased savings potential. Here are some of the details:

- All contributions are tax-deductible and, like a personal IRA, earnings on investments accumulate tax deferred until withdrawn at retirement.

- If you are an employee of your company, you can contribute up to 15 percent of your salary or $24,000, whichever is less. As a sole proprietor, the amount you can contribute is lower because you have to use a complicated IRS formula that requires you to add half of your self-employment tax back to your taxable business income.

• You can change the percentage you want to contribute and you can even skip a year, making no contribution at all. This allows you the flexibility to decide how much you want to contribute each year, adjusting to accommodate boom and lean years.

• If you hire other employees, you must offer them the option of participating in the SEP program once they earn at least $400 per year for three of the past five years.

• You do not have to file any annual reports with the IRS after you set up a SEP IRA.

• To set up a SEP IRA you must establish the account with a financial institution and file IRS Form 5305-SEP or 5305A-SEP. You can set up a SEP anytime before your IRS taxes are due. If you are a sole proprietor, that's any time on or before the date your federal taxes are due. If you are incorporated, it's anytime on or before March 15 plus extensions.

Keogh

Keogh plans are more complicated and require more paper-work than either personal IRAs or SEPs. If you maximize your Keogh plan, you can save up to 25 percent of your income. Here are the details:

There are two options to Keogh plans: profit-sharing and money-purchase. You can elect to set up the money-purchase option by itself or you can combine both options. The profit-sharing option is very similar to a SEP IRA. You can contribute up to 15 percent of your net earnings, you set how much you want to contribute every year, and you can skip an annual contribution. Although you can contribute up to an additional 10 percent with the money-purchase option, it is much less flexible because once you declare the percentage you will contribute, you must contribute that amount every year.

As an employee of your company, you can contribute up to 25 percent of your taxable business income or $30,000, whichever is less. However, as a sole proprietor, the amount you can contribute is lower because you have to use the same IRS formula required for a SEP where you add half of your self-employment tax back to your taxable business income.

You can also combine a Keogh money-purchase plan with a SEP-IRA in the same way you would combine a Keogh money-purchase with a Keogh profit-sharing plan. The same rules apply for maximum contributions and handling of the self-employment tax for sole proprietors.

Because of the added paperwork and maintenance, not every financial institution provides Keogh plans. Each year you or your representative must file an informational return with the IRS (Form 5500). To set up a Keogh plan, check with a qualified financial advisor.

SIMPLE

In August 1996, the government enacted the Small Business Job Protection Act. Part of that legislation included a new retirement plan called the Savings Incentive Match Plan for Employees (SIMPLE). Congress designed the plan to make it easier for small employers to offer a retirement plan for their employees. Here are the details.

- You must have 100 or fewer employees to qualify.

- As an employee of your business, you can make pretax salary deferred contributions to the account up to the lesser of $6,000 or 100 percent of your compensation.

- As an employer, you are required to either match individual employee contributions up to 3 percent of the employee's pay or make an across-the-board contribution equal to 2 percent of all employees' pay, even if some employees elect not to make any contributions of their own.

- The government does not require you to file any reports or tax returns with the IRS or the Department of Labor.

Although SIMPLE plans are relatively new, they require much less paperwork than a Keogh or 401(k) plan. Many financial institutions should have the appropriate paperwork to establish a SIMPLE plan.

Other retirement plans

In addition to the retirement plans discussed above, you can also create a 401(k) plan or have an attorney customize a plan for your business. Some financial institutions (banks, brokerage firms,

ISSUE	Standard IRA (deductible & nondeductible)	ROTH IRA	SEP	KEOGH		SIMPLE
				Profit Sharing	Money Purchase	
What is the annual limit on contributions?	Lesser of 100% of earned income or $2,000 max	Lesser of 100% of earned income or $2,000 max	15% of compensation up to $24,000 per year	15% of compensation up to $24,000 per year	25% of compensation up to $30,000 per year	Lesser of 100% of compensation or $6,000 (pre tax) per year
Annual contributions required?	No	No	No	No	Yes	Yes
What are participant requirements?	Except for unemployed spouse, must have earned income	Except for unemployed spouse, must have earned income	Maximum requirements: 3 years of service out of the last 5 years, age 21, and earns at least $400 annually	Maximum requirement are 2 years of service at 1,000 hours/ year and age 21	Maximum requirements are 2 years of service at 1,000 hours/ year and age 21	Maximum requirements: 2 years of service with minimum earnings of $5,000 in each of any 2 prior years
How are contributions and benefits determined?	Deductible amount based on earned income caps	Deductible amount based on earned income caps	Determined annually by the employer	Determined annually by the employer	Based on fixed percentage of employee's compensation	Employer must either: (1) match 3% of participating employee's pay, or (2) contribute 2% of all employees pay
When must contributions be made?	By April 15	By April 15	By employer's tax filing due date plus extensions	By employer's tax filing due date plus extensions	By employer's tax filing due date plus extensions	On a salary reduction basis. Employer contributions by tax filing due date plus extensions
Are qualified distributions taxable?	Yes*	No	Yes	Yes	Yes	Yes
How complex is plan to set up?	Easy	Easy	Easy	Hard	Hard	Easy

*Nondeductible contributions are not taxed.

Table 8-1: Types of retirement plans

and so forth) have prototype plans for 401(k) or other types of plans that can provide a template for your own specialized plan. These types of plans are typically more appropriate for larger companies with more than 75 employees. They are more expensive to set up and require more paperwork to maintain. If you feel these types of plans are appropriate for your situation, consult a qualified attorney or financial planner to help you set one up.

Summary of plans

The table on the previous page provides a summary of the types of government-approved retirement plans.

Tips for Setting Up Your Home Office

9

"He [Robert Benchley] and I had an office so tiny that an inch smaller and it would have been adultery."

—Dorothy Parker (1893–1967), U.S. humorous writer
interview in *Writers at Work* (1958)

When people ask me about the consulting business, their eyes light up when they ask about the possibility of working at home. Your home office offers the possibility to avoid the daily commute, get more work done, and be closer to your family. Unlike an office or cubicle provided to you by an employer, you get to pick the kind of space you want and you don't have to get permission to outfit it with the tools you need to do your job. Your home office may be the place where you do your most creative and productive work. This chapter provides some tips for setting up communications and computer equipment. It also discusses deducting your home office as a business expense.

Since you may spend considerable time in your home office, select your space wisely. The goal for setting up a home office is to create an efficient work environment separate from your private life. Find a space conducive to your work habits. Do you prefer lots of natural light? If so, find a room or section of the house near a window. Assess the space for availability of power outlets and phone jacks. Make sure the space you select has plenty of storage space and room for your equipment, supplies, file cabinets, books, desk, and so forth—not only for today, but for future expansion.

The space you select should be quiet and removed from distractions. If possible, try to find a separate room with a door. Besides making it easier to justify the space for a home office deduction, it allows you to close the door and get work done while other family members occupy the house. If a separate room is not available, use a screen or some other divider to separate your office space. This cuts down on noise and clearly identifies the space to your family.

Many home-based businesses decide to put their home office in their basement either by design or out of necessity. If you intend to do the same, I suggest you consider this decision very carefully. Basements can flood and it only takes one such incident to wipe out your electrical equipment and your paper records. If the basement is your only choice, make sure everything is high off the floor. Also, if possible, add flood insurance to your business equipment insurance.

Communications

To provide the most flexible system for you to communicate with your clients, employees, and business associates, you must create a flexible communication system that keeps you in touch without discouraging people from contacting you. To cover all the potential communication mediums, you should have fax, email, and telephone capabilities. Here are some basic tips.

Get a separate phone line for your business. When you run your business from your home, you need to separate your personal calls from your business calls. This separates your business answering messages from your personal ones and provides you with an independent telephone bill for your business. With a separate business phone bill, you can track your business phone costs and keep track of your phone time with clients.

Use an offsite answering system. I suggest you contract with your telephone company or other service provider to handle your voice messages through a separate offsite system. If you don't answer a call within a preset number of rings, the telephone company or service provider plays your outgoing message and records any messages. Services can include multiple voice mail message boxes for multiple employees. The advantage of these systems is that they maintain the equipment and continue to record messages even if several clients call at the same time.

Using an answering machine to handle your calls has many disadvantages. If the machine malfunctions, you may miss important calls. While one client is leaving a message, another client calling at the same time cannot connect with your business.

Some people like the idea of getting a computer interface card that acts as a telephone answering system. However, in addition to all the problems shared with an answering machine, these cards require you to keep your PC powered 24 hours a day.

The one advantage of an answering machine is the ability to screen calls by listening to who is calling before you answer the phone. But with a caller-ID device, you can see who calls before you decide to answer.

Get a multiline telephone or phone service. While you are doing business at home, you may still need to answer calls on your personal phone line. Since desk space is usually at a premium in a home office, you can access both lines by getting a multiline telephone in which you switch to the line you want to answer. Also, with two lines and the right multiline phone, you will always have three-way conference capabilities when you and two other callers need to talk to one another. If you don't want to maintain this functionality in your phone, many telephone companies offer the ability to answer two telephone numbers on one physical line by varying the sound of the telephone's ring. Most telephone companies also offer three-way calling on one line for teleconferencing with two other parties.

Get a telephone headset. Keep your hands free while you engage in cold calling or long conversations with clients. This frees you to take notes or type into your computer while you talk. If you get a headset with a cordless transmitter, you can roam the house while you conduct your business, tending to children or household chores.

Get a cell phone or beeper. If you are managing several projects while on the move, you should consider getting a cell phone or beeper to guarantee a more timely connection with clients, employees, and business associates.

Use a fax service to receive your faxes. You can set up a fax mailbox that receives your faxes offsite in the same way an email account receives your email messages. This service is offered by some local telephone companies and by other service providers. These services provide you a telephone number that you use as your fax phone number. A fax mailbox allows you to receive faxes 24 hours a day, 7 days a week, without leaving your computer or fax machine running. This saves you the cost of adding an additional line for your fax machine or purchasing equipment that lets you share your fax with your voice line. Unlike a fax machine, several people can transmit faxes to you at the same time without getting a busy signal.

Get email. Electronic mail is increasingly replacing paper mail as the preferred written communication between businesses and individuals. In addition to the speed of delivery, email has many other advantages. You can broadcast a message to many users, perhaps even create an electronic newsletter for your clients. You can attach electronic documents such as your resume or a report for a client. Email is becoming so commonplace in business that if you do not have it, you risk looking peculiar to your clients and colleagues.

Computer equipment

Regardless of the type of independent consulting you engage in, a computer system is one essential tool you cannot do without. Even if you are not consulting in a technical field, you will need a computer to handle your correspondence, email, invoices, payroll, and other critical business functions. It is beyond the scope of this book to recommend specific brands of computer equipment because of the wide variation in models and technology. Regardless of the type of computer equipment you purchase, here are some key tips.

Purchase a computer near the top of the product line. The goal is to purchase a system that provides you with excess capacity. When you need to purchase a new computer, you want to get one that can provide you with at least three years of service before you need a new system. You should purchase a system in the middle or near the top of the product line. Avoid inexpensive computers sold at the bottom of the product line. Your savings will be short-lived when software upgrades quickly outstrip the capacity of that bargain basement PC you purchased six months ago.

Consider upgrading only your system motherboard. The parts of your computer system that go through the least frequent technological change are the monitor and computer case. So, if all you need is a faster system, why replace these items? You can replace the guts of your computer (the motherboard) at a fraction of the cost of replacing an entire system. This may make it easier to purchase the fastest system available, because you're not paying for parts you don't need. Although superstore distributors of entire systems will avoid this kind of work, many independent computer stores make their living providing system upgrades as a service.

When space is a premium, combine functions. If you need to conserve space in your home office, you might consider multi-function equipment. Hewlett-Packard and others offer devices that combine a copier, scanner, fax machine, and printer all in one unit. Although you will gain in space, you might have to compromise on features. To fit all those components into one device for a reasonable price, many manufacturers had to cut back on advanced features that you may find on separate devices. That means you may have to do without reduction capability on a copier or accept a lower dot-per-inch (DPI) printer. Also, if one part of the device breaks down, you lose use of the other functions while it's being repaired.

Consider media exchange options. If you need to exchange electronic information you should consider what media you need to exchange large files with clients and/or colleagues. With the size of documents and graphics growing exponentially, you may need a device that handles media with a larger capacity than a 3¼-inch diskette can deliver.

There are many choices of magnetic media devices that can store large amounts of information on a single medium. In addition to traditional magnetic media, the cost of CD-ROM writers continues to drop. CD-Record (CD-R) and CD-Rewrite (CD-RW) drives both provide 650 MB of space. You can only record information on CD-R media, but any recently manufactured CD-ROM drive can read a CD-R disk. Although you can write and erase many times to CD-RW media, only CD-ROM drives specially equipped for CD-RW media can read CD-RW disks.

Get an uninterruptible power supply (UPS). This device provides battery backup power to your computer equipment in the event of a power loss. This is relatively cheap insurance against lost client files or damaged equipment. Most units only provide 5 to 10 minutes of power during a power loss, but this is enough time to close your computer files and properly power-down your equipment to avoid potential disk drive damage.

Make backup easier. Considering the value of the information you store on your computer, it is shocking how many independent consultants don't back up their computer data. You *must* regularly back up your essential files and properly store your backups to avoid a business disaster. I suggest you back up your data at least once a week. Make the job easier by selecting a backup media that can back up your essential files with a minimum of media swapping. Select a tape or removable disk drive with a large enough capacity to contain all your key data on one tape or disk so the backup runs uninterrupted without waiting for you to insert another media before finishing. Store your backup separate from your computer in a fire-resistant container.

Deducting your home office

Although there has been a great deal of confusion and paranoia surrounding the home office deduction, you may decide it's appropriate to use it. Here are some considerations.

C corporations need not apply. Only sole proprietors filing IRS Schedule C and S corporations qualify for the home office deduction. C corporations do not qualify.

Basic requirements. IRS Publication 587 describes the requirements for deducting expenses related to the business use of part of your home. To qualify to claim expenses for the business use of your home, you must meet the following requirements.

Your use must be:

Exclusive. You must use a specific area of your home only for your trade or business. The area used for business can be a room or other separate space. The space does not need to be marked off by a permanent partition. You do not meet the requirements of the exclusive use test if you use the area in question for both business and personal purposes.

Regular. You must use a specific area of your home for business on a continuing basis. You do not meet the test if your business use of the area is only occasional or incidental, even if you do not use that area for any other purpose.

For your trade or business. You must use part of your home in connection with a trade or business. If you use your home for a profit-seeking activity that is not a trade or business, you cannot take a deduction for its business use.

In addition to all of the above criteria, the business part of your home must be *one* of the following:

- Your principal place of business for your trade or business, *or*

- A place of business where you meet or deal with patients, clients, or customers in the normal course of your trade or business, *or*

- A separate structure (not attached to your home) that you use in connection with your trade or business.

Use IRS Form 8829. This form, titled *Expenses for Business Use of Your Home,* steps you through the calculations necessary to establish the business use of your home. This form is required in conjunction with your Schedule C or S corporation tax return.

Related deductions. Once you establish your qualifications for the home office deduction, you calculate your business percentage on Form 8829. You then use this business percentage to calculate deductions for items such as real estate taxes, deductible mortgage interest, casualty losses, rent, insurance, depreciation (if you own your home), repairs, security system, and utilities and services.

Selling your house. The biggest problem with the home office deduction is that when you sell your house you are liable to reimburse the IRS for the depreciation deduction you've taken while living in your home. Currently, the IRS sets the depreciation recapture tax at 25 percent of the total depreciation deduction you've taken all the years you've filed Form 8829. You report the depreciation recapture tax on Form 1040, Schedule D.

Marketing Strategies

> *"Grace is given of God, but knowledge is bought in the market."*
>
> —Arthur Hugh Clough (1819–1861), British poet

Marketing is the ability to communicate the value of your consulting services to a wide audience of potential clients. Marketing skills are the most important skills you need to succeed as an independent consultant. Without them, no one knows you exist and your business will wither in isolation.

To succeed at marketing you must possess better-than-average communications skills because to get your message across you must communicate with confidence, verbally, visually, and in writing. If necessary, you can get help with some of these skills. You can hire someone to help you write copy for a brochure and a graphic artist to design the visual presentation. But some skills, like writing a marketing cover letter and making a presentation, you'll have to learn yourself. Even here, you can get help through sales seminars or by joining an organization such as Toastmasters, which provides practice giving presentations.

In this chapter, I'll discuss some common marketing strategies and outlets for your marketing message. I've roughly divided these strategies into two types: *passive* techniques that emphasize your written skills and *active* techniques that emphasize your verbal and presentation skills.

Basic principles

Before we discuss specific marketing strategies, let's take a look at some basic marketing principles.

Focus attention on strategies that pay off

Marketing is not an end unto itself. You want your marketing efforts to reach the appropriate clients with the minimal effort. Concentrate your efforts on putting your ideas in front of people who buy your brand of consulting services. Change your marketing strategy if you find you're spending too much time marketing to the wrong group of people.

Market continuously

Marketing is like a garden that requires perpetual care. You must constantly prune and weed your marketing strategy. Although it will go against every instinct in your body, the best time to market is when you don't need the work. Use prosperous times to build a pipeline of business for down times.

Be patient

It takes time for marketing to work, especially since so much depends on word-of-mouth. It will probably take at least six to eight months of hardcore marketing before you get a steady stream of clients.

Promote positive word-of-mouth

Positive word-of-mouth is always your best salesperson. Everything you do from the way you answer the phone to the work you deliver must leave the people you contact with a positive impression of you. The best byproduct of providing high-quality service is the recommendation of a satisfied client. Many satisfied clients will go out of their way to recommend you to their colleagues. Encourage them to spread the word. Solicit positive quotes and letters of referral from your clients.

Don't forget to use your network of friends and family. You might be surprised to find that many of them work at companies that are in the market for your services or know of someone else who is. When you start your consulting business, tell all your friends what you do and encourage them to keep an eye out for any potential opportunities.

Be prepared

Marketing opportunities come in different packages. You never know when you will meet a potential client. It could be at a wedding or a funeral. It could be at your health club or riding on the bus. Be prepared. Always carry your business cards with you. Reduce a description of your business to one or two sentences and practice delivering this description so it becomes second nature. For example, I use the following description for my consulting business: "I'm a technical writer. I design and write paper and online documentation for computer software."

Use both passive and active marketing techniques

Most marketing techniques fall into one of two categories: passive or active. The following sections describe these two categories of marketing techniques.

Passive marketing techniques

Passive marketing techniques are any techniques that do not require your personal interaction while they are working. Some examples follow.

Membership directories

As mentioned earlier, by joining a professional organization, you get your name in the organization's directory. This is often your best advertising. Some organizations, particularly those made up of independent consultants, allow you to describe your business in the directory. Independent consultant organizations also actively distribute copies of their directory to potential industry clients. Try to include as much contact information as possible so potential clients have many ways to reach you. This includes your address, phone number, email, and Web site address.

Resource guides

To make them more valuable as a reference, many industry publications include special sections that categorize and list industry vendors. Some simply provide a listing of Web site addresses while others allow the vendor to provide a paragraph describing their services. Often these publications offer this service to vendors without charge or as a free benefit of your subscription. Others charge a fee to list in their resource guide, but at substantially lower rates than what you would pay for a display ad.

Survey your industry publications to find those that provide resource guides. Find out which ones include listings as part of your subscription and which charge for listing in their resource guide, then target your subscription and advertising dollars accordingly. Even if a well-distributed publication charges for listing in its resource guide, this form of advertising can provide an inexpensive alternative to display ads in a popular publication.

Certified vendor listings

Many industry vendors provide a certification program for consultants who use their products. This is quite prevalent in the computer industry where companies like Microsoft, Adobe, and Novell maintain industry recognized certification programs. These programs usually provide some form of referral system for graduates of their certification program. The level of assistance a vendor provides varies. Some vendors simply list you in their directory of certified professionals while others actively refer clients to you.

If you plan to get certified on a vendor product to increase your credentials, assess the vendor's referral program for certified professionals. Ask the vendor if they provide their clients a listing of certified professionals and if they directly refer clients. You may decide that it's better to get certified by the number two vendor with an active referral program rather than the number one vendor who only provides a listing to customers on request. Of course, if you can afford it, you could complete both certification programs to cover all the bases. Check the Recommended Resources section of this book for Web sites and books about certification programs.

Web page

The Web provides a huge marketing opportunity for independent consultants, provided your target client uses this technology.

A Web page offers potential clients your brochure, on demand, 24 hours a day. As of this writing, many online services and Internet Service Providers (ISPs) offer several megabytes of storage to host your own Web page as part of your service fee.

If you are already using the Web through an ISP or online service such as CompuServe or America Online, ask them what type of services they offer as part of your monthly fee to host your Web page. See Chapter 12 for more information about marketing on the Web.

Print advertising

Although print advertising in major publications is often priced too high for most independent consultants, there are less expensive methods. For example, as a member of a professional organization, you may get a special rate to place an ad in the organization's periodical.

There are some potential problems with print advertising. For one thing, you have to select publications targeted at your potential clients. If you select too general a publication, you waste time filtering clients who want services you don't provide. Another risk with print advertising is that you could become a victim of your own success. Your ad may attract so many qualified clients at one time that your business becomes overwhelmed. As mentioned above, if the publication has a resource listing, you may want to consider this as an alternative to a display ad in the same publication.

Yellow Pages

You might consider placing a listing in your local Yellow Pages, but be prepared for the expense. You'll also have to select an appropriate category or categories that your clients are most likely to look in when they need your services. You may want to be listed in more than one category, but often the second category is less expensive. As veteran consultant Candace Masella points out, "In my experience, a Yellow Pages listing is expensive, but people use it. Don't count on the directory publisher to help you classify your listing. Think like your potential clients, then look through the Yellow Pages for the right category."

Mass mailing

Although risky and potentially expensive, mass mailing may have a place in your marketing plan. The key to a successful mass mailing campaign is to have a good, targeted list. You can build a list from your own contacts or purchase a list from a mailing list broker. Check the Yellow Pages or search the Web to find list brokers.

You can control your costs by mailing postcards instead of letters. Postcards also save the recipient the trouble of having to decide if they want to open the mail piece or not. You have a better chance they will read your message before it's tossed in the trash. If you feel restrained by the small space that postcards afford, remember that you can always refer the reader to your Web site for more details.

Referral bulletin boards

Many professional organizations (particularly those dedicated to independent consultants) operate referral bulletin boards for their members. This can take the form of a telephone hotline, Web page, or local computer bulletin board. Most of these referral systems work by encouraging potential clients to post job orders on the bulletin board system for free. Then, members check the bulletin board and respond either directly to the client or to the professional organization, who then contacts the client. Some of these organizations charge their members a fee for this service (usually a percentage of the revenue from the project); others provide it free.

The key to using a referral service is the reputation it has with industry clients. If the organization makes some effort to screen its members so a client can count on getting a quality consultant, then clients will continue to use the service. However, if the organization's requirements are lax and they attract less qualified people who join only to exploit the referral service, then clients lose confidence in the system and stop using the service. Despite this caveat, if you qualify to join a professional organization and they offer a referral service, it doesn't hurt to participate, especially if the service is free to you.

Cross-business promotions

Perhaps you can enter into a mutual system of referrals with a complementary field. For example, in my field of technical communication it's common for technical writers to refer graphic artists, indexers, and trainers and vice versa.

Make sure any agreement you get into with another business is fair and balanced. You don't want to take on a second job being the salesperson for another business and getting nothing in return. Make sure you are really selecting a *complementary* business and not just some generic consumer business that is trying to pump you for your client list. It makes sense for a programmer and technical writer to refer business to each other; however, a programmer and an insurance salesperson may not be a good match. Technically, everyone the programmer meets is a potential client for the insurance salesperson, but the insurance salesperson will rarely meet someone who needs commercial programming services unless he or she specializes in selling insurance to software companies.

Nonprofit promotions

Many nonprofit organizations publish directories of their business supporters or mention businesses that contribute to their cause. For instance, the public radio station in my area publishes a Business Partners Directory that includes a brief description of your business, your address, and phone number for a reasonable donation. Some alumni associations also publish directories and/or allow alumni to put ads in their newsletters.

If there is a special nonprofit organization that you plan to support anyway, it may not hurt to take advantage of any publicity benefits they offer. You might be giving up a targeted audience to be included with all other types of businesses. But, depending on the cost, if you snag even one client with this method, it could pay for itself while you help a cause you care about at the same time.

Active marketing techniques

Active marketing techniques require your personal interaction for them to work. Some people consider these true sales activities because you are directly soliciting business from potential clients.

Networking

Networking could be your best active marketing technique. The *National Business Employment Weekly's* book *Networking* describes networking as "the systematic development and cultivation of informal interpersonal contacts and relationships...." Networking is a somewhat subtle art that probably lies somewhere between casual conversation and outright promotion or salesmanship. The primary method of networking is talking one-on-one to someone in person or over the phone. Typically, you will network in some sponsored forum such as professional organizations, conventions, classrooms, seminars, and basically any place where people in your field collect.

In addition to networking in organizations where you expect to find your peers, you might consider joining organizations where you might find your clients. For example, a programmer who is a member of the Independent Computer Consultants Association (ICCA) may also join the Data Processing Managers Association (DPMA), the Software Publishers Association (SPA), the Association of Systems Managers (ASM), and the Microcomputer Managers Association (MMA). Even if you do not qualify to join these type of organizations directly, you can usually attend their regularly scheduled program meetings as a nonmember.

You will do different kinds of networking depending on where you conduct the networking. Sometimes your networking goal is to solicit new business and other times you will network simply to increase the size of your network. When you network at an independent consultant event, you want to get tips to run your business and to build a referral network. When you network at a convention or client professional organization, you are trying to find new business. Here is some "netiquette" for networking.

Do's:

- Continue networking when you're busy. As with all your marketing activities, you must continue networking even when business is good.

- Dress appropriately. Dress right for the occasion. Wear business attire for a program meeting or convention; dress casual for a picnic; wear business or casual clothing for a class or seminar.

- Always carry your business cards with you. At a minimum, be ready to give out your business card if someone you talk to asks for it. You might also want to tuck away a copy of your resume and/or brochure. I suggest you do not offer these last two unless the person you are talking to specifically asks for them. Otherwise, you may come off as being pushy. A better strategy might be to carry only your business cards, using the request for more detailed materials as an excuse to contact the person again outside of the networking forum.

- Ask people about their business. This not only keeps you from always talking about yourself, but provides you with information about their business situation.

- Write notes on the back of other people's business cards. If someone requested more information about your business, write what they wanted on the back of their card. Also write down where you met them.

- Volunteer to help. One of the best ways to network is to volunteer to assist the organization where you do most of your networking. This gives you a higher profile in the organization, allows you to meet with organization insiders, and builds your credentials.

Don'ts:

- Don't talk only about yourself. Remember, listening is your business' most important input. Pace yourself, let the other person talk, and pay attention!

- Don't become a "black hole." A black hole sucks all the energy in and gives nothing back. Don't use networking to get free consulting on how to run your business or to pump someone for referrals.

- Don't complain. No one wants to hear a complainer who whines about how badly they need new business. You won't get business by trying to make people feel sorry for you.

- Don't "push" marketing materials. Don't walk up to a stranger with one hand extended for a handshake and the other hand holding your business card and resume. If someone wants to know how to reach you or get more information, you will get some indication or they will simply ask for it. Wait for the right signal.

- Avoid discussing politics or religion with someone you don't know well. Unless you are networking at a political or religious forum with like-minded people, it's best to hold off expressing your stand on these issues until you get to know the person better.

Career fairs

Job or career fairs offer another active marketing opportunity, particularly for skills contracting. Check the job section of your local paper for any mention of job or career fairs for your industry. These events offer you the chance to talk with companies who need additional resources for their business.

Prepare a short resume and/or list of successfully completed projects. Make sure you place on your resume, somewhere near the top in bold type, the words "Contract _____ (insert the term for your profession)." For example, in my case I would put Contract Technical Writer. You don't want your resume to be confused with those applying for a permanent position in the company. Your goal is not necessarily to get a project right away, but to make contact with a company and get information about your services into their hands, so that when the need arises, they can contact you.

Try to get a list of the companies that will exhibit at the career fair, then target the companies you want to contact. For example, you may decide you don't want to waste your time talking with any agencies, preferring to develop more direct clients. Make sure you give yourself plenty of time to speak with all your target companies. Exhibiting companies typically spend the last half hour of the last day of a career fair packing up their materials and breaking down their display, so they will not be available to talk.

When you introduce yourself, explain that you are an independent consultant and you wish to offer your services on a contract basis. When you do this, you will get one of several reactions:

"We don't hire contractors." Some companies have strict policies of never hiring contractors, only permanent employees. In this case, all you can do is thank them and move on to another booth.

"Are you interested in a permanent position?" Don't be surprised if a company tries to lure you into a permanent position. As an expert independent consultant, you're a good catch for a company looking to hire the best. Of course, you can always consider this, but if you are truly committed to your independent consulting business, you should be flattered and politely explain you would like to remain independent for now.

Some companies have a difficult time filling permanent positions when there is a shortage of people available with a particular skill. Sometimes this holds up completion of a particular project. If this is the case, you can suggest they consider hiring you to keep the project moving forward while they continue to search for a permanent employee. You can even offer to help them find a qualified candidate as an additional, value-added service while you work on the project.

"I'm not sure where to submit your resume." One disadvantage of career fairs from a contractor's point of view is that when you go to the booth of a larger company, you will probably talk to someone from the human resources (HR) department. Since these events are usually organized with the intention of snagging a permanent employee, I've discovered often that the HR departments of some companies don't know how to handle resumes from contractors. When I introduce myself I sometimes get a blank stare as the person operating the booth tries to figure out what "channel" in the company should receive the resume. If you know your industry well enough, you can usually suggest specific departments to which the HR person can pass along your resume.

This is much less of a problem with small and medium companies that don't have HR departments and may even have the CEO manning their booth. These companies are usually very receptive to a resume from a contractor even if they don't have any current needs for your services.

"We don't currently have a need for a contractor." Even if a company does not have a current need for your business, explain to them you want to make them aware that you offer these services should they need you in the future. Most companies who do not have a restriction against contractors will still include your resume in their files.

Cold calling

The problem with passive marketing techniques is that it usually takes time for them to create new business for you. So what do you do when you need business right now? The answer is cold calling. Cold calling is a sales activity in which you contact (usually over the phone) someone who does not know you and attempt to sell them your services.

No one likes cold calling. I worked for two sales organizations where I met dozens of salespeople and I never met one who liked cold calling. Most did everything they could to avoid it, preferring to sell to their existing customers instead. There is something about the repetitive rejection characteristic of cold calling that triggers the "fight or flight" response in most people.

Cold calling does, however, produce results. As much as I dislike the activity myself, I've often gotten new business immediately through cold calling. Remember, somewhere out there, right this moment, there is a manager sitting at his or her desk with a project to complete and insufficient in-house resources. They're waiting for your call! The smartest way to approach cold calling is to accept that you will dislike the experience and arm yourself with good strategies. Here's some tips for successful cold calling:

Compile a good prospect list. As with mass mailing, you increase the potential success of your cold calling effort by using a targeted prospect list rather than a shotgun approach. One of the best ways to do this is to start your cold calling as a networking activity. Call your current clients and ask them if they can give you the names of any colleagues who may need your services. This activity accomplishes three things. First, it builds your cold calling prospect list. Second, it provides an introduction to those prospects when you call them. Third, it helps maintain your relationship with your current clients. You may also uncover new opportunities at your current clients in the process.

Other sources of prospects include the following:
- Directories from professional organizations.
- Industry advertisements.
- Yellow Page listings for your field.
- Internet search engines.
- Conventions/trade show mailing lists.
- Industry publication mailing lists.
- Business news stories.

Narrow your pitch. Cold calling works best if you can narrowly define your services. For example, as a technical writer, I do better at cold calling if I propose specific paper and online help documentation rather than general "technical communication" services.

Set cold calling objectives. Successful cold calling is a numbers game. You have to make many successful connections to produce new business. Set a specific day and time to cold call and the number of successful connections you will make. What is a "successful" connection? Consider a connection successful if you either talk directly to a decision maker or decision influencer or can leave a verbal message on their answering system. As you will learn later, leaving a message can serve as your verbal business card.

Define a successful outcome. To make cold calling easier to handle, remember that you do not have to measure your outcome by how many prospects you persuaded to hire you on the spot. Instead, your goal should be to build a new relationship with someone who will want your service at some time. "Some time" may be immediately or a month from now. As such, there are three successful outcomes to your cold calling.

The first and best outcome is scheduling a meeting with the prospect. Even if the client does not have a particular project in mind at this time, it's always a good idea to try and schedule a face-to-face meeting to describe your services and leave behind your marketing materials. If you can't schedule a meeting with the client, the second best outcome is a request for your marketing materials. The third best outcome occurs when the prospect admits that he or she cannot use your services, but refers you to other colleagues who can.

Pace yourself. When you call a prospect, limit the small talk. Remember, you have a lot of calls to make and their time is precious. When you complete a call, keep going! Dial the next number without replacing the handset. If you put the phone down, you risk breaking your stride and becoming distracted by a less intimidating activity. You might want to consider purchasing a telephone headset. This will make the calls more comfortable and leaves both hands free to write or type notes.

Use a script. It's normal to be nervous when you're cold calling. Because of this, it's not a good idea to talk off the top of your head when explaining your services. The person listening to you will allow you a very narrow time slot in which to keep his attention, so you don't want to blow what little time you have by being unprepared. The best way to keep from stumbling when you call is to use a prewritten script. You will use two kinds of scripts: a live script for talking directly to a prospect and a voice mail script for when you leave a message. Figures 10-1 and 10-2 provide an example of a live cold calling script and an example of a script for a voice mail message.

I suggest you practice your scripts by reciting them into a recording device and playing them back. You can also practice your scripts on a cooperative friend or colleague.

Public speaking

Another active marketing technique is public speaking. Public speaking is also a high profile method of networking. Public speaking is probably more terrifying to most people than cold calling, so you may want to start with a small group at first.

One of the best places to start is a program meeting at a professional organization or one of their Special Interest Groups (SIG). Some organizations book their speakers far in advance, but many

You:	Hi! I'm hoping you can help me. I'm trying to reach the person in your company who is in charge of technical publications such as software user manuals, product documentation, or training materials.
Prospect:	What is this regarding?
You:	I operate a technical communication consulting company and would like to discuss my company's services.
If connected:	Hi! I was told you are the person in charge of documentation (and training) for _____. Is that correct?
If no, continue search.	
If yes:	My name is _____. I have a technical writing and consulting company called _____. We design and write technical documentation. I was calling to see if your company has planned any documentation projects that you might consider outsourcing.
If not at this time:	Do you see a need for this type of service in the next six to eight months?
If yes:	If it's okay with you, I'd like to send you a list of our project experience and some writing samples. Then we can talk again after you've had a chance to review those materials.
If no:	Do you know of anyone else who might need help completing a documentation project? Perhaps another department or colleague?
If maybe:	If it's okay with you, I'd like to send you a list of our project experience and a few pages of writing samples. That way, you'll have something on file when the need arises.
Confirm name and address.	
Closing:	Thank you for your time.

Figure 10-1: Sample live cold-calling script

Hello, my name is _____. I have a technical writing and consulting company called _____. We design and write computer or product documentation and training materials. I was calling to see if your company has any projects that could benefit from these services.

If you are interested in receiving a list of our project experience and a few pages of writing samples, you can reach me at _____. You can also download samples of our work at our Web site at _____. Once again, my name is _____ and my company is _____. Thank you.

Figure 10-2: Sample voice mail script

are desperately looking to fill gaps in their programs with relevant presentations. If a group to whom you want to speak shows interest in your subject, but does not have an open slot in the near future, ask to be considered a "backup" speaker in the event one of their regular speakers cancels. However, if you agree to be a backup speaker, make sure you have your presentation prepared ahead of time.

If you are booked to speak to a group, make sure you publicize the event. Don't depend on the organization itself to thoroughly publicize your talk. No doubt, they will inform their immediate members, but there are other groups outside the organization that may be interested in hearing what you have to say. Here are some ideas for publicizing your talk:

- Send a letter, postcard, or email to your clients and any potential prospects.

- Send a notice to any local papers that publish a calendar of upcoming events. Include who, what, where, when, cost (if any), and event contact information.

- Update your Web page to describe the subject, when, where, and how to sign up for your presentation.

- Post information about your presentation in Internet newsgroups and online forums.

Seminars and teaching

Another high profile active marketing technique is to leverage your expert status by presenting seminars or teaching a class. In addition to acting as a method of marketing, seminars and teaching can be another source of revenue for your business.

Seminars are typically short, running anywhere from one hour to two weeks. Because of this, seminars usually feature a tightly focused subject. You can create a seminar of your own or try to become a contract instructor for a training company. The advantage of creating your own seminar is that you control the material and collect all the money. Also, there is no problem using the seminar to promote your consulting business. When you contract to a training company, you not only make less money, but the training company may impose restrictions on your marketing activities.

Typically, when you teach a class, you deal with a more general subject taught over a longer period of time at an educational institution. Many for-credit institutions require credentialed instructors to teach their classes. You can avoid this problem by shooting for a noncredit course taught to students in the institution's continuing education program. Some of these institutions seek instructors to teach courses already in their program, while others are open to new courses proposed by you. If you decide to propose a course, keep in mind that these institutions schedule their programs far in advance, so don't propose a subject that's irrelevant when the institution actually schedules the course. Also, check the institution's policy on promoting your business in their classroom.

Interface Materials

"A worker may be the hammer's master, but the hammer still prevails. A tool knows exactly how it is meant to be handled, while the user of the tool can only have an approximate idea."

—Milan Kundera (1929–), Czech author, critic
The Book of Laughter and Forgetting.

What are the standard marketing tools of the independent consultant? Even if you're new to consulting, you've probably already used one marketing tool in your career: your resume. You're probably also familiar with brochures and business cards, even if it's only on the receiving end. Less obvious marketing tools include invoices, checks, portfolios, and pitch books. In her book, *The Computer Consultant's Guide*, Janet Ruhl calls these marketing tools "interface materials."

Interface materials have several functions. They act as reinforcers, provide background, and let clients know how to reach you. Remember, these materials represent your business when you're not around. You never know where they will end up. Besides your direct distribution, your clients may pass on your marketing materials to their colleagues. So don't underestimate the importance of well-designed paper-based marketing tools.

When designing paper-based marketing tools, you can chose predesigned materials or have them custom made by a graphic artist. The low initial cost and flexibility of predesigned materials is particularly attractive in the early years of your business. You will make many changes to your content during the first few years of business as you experiment with different marketing strategies. At some point you may want to create a truly unique look for your business by contracting with a graphic artist to design custom materials.

Letterhead

You will use your letterhead or stationery for all your written paper correspondence. Of course, the exact content of each letter you send will be different, but you should set aside space on your letterhead to serve as a billboard for your business. In addition to all the standard contact information (address, phone number, fax, email, Web address, and so forth) you can include a list of your services and your logo.

Envelopes

Envelopes provide an opportunity to communicate something more than your return name and address. There are several ways you can spice up your envelopes to make them stand out. This is particularly important when you mass mail marketing information and you want to increase the chances that the recipient will open the envelope. However, you don't want your envelopes to look like one from a sweepstakes promotion. To maintain your professional image, limit the amount of blatant advertising you display on your envelope.

You could print a company tag line like the one Gateway computers uses: "You've got a friend in the business." You could also use your envelopes to communicate new company news such as "Visit our new Web site at Consulting.com!" You could also alert the recipient to a promotional discount with, "Your first two consulting hours free! See inside for details."

You can print extra information on either the front, back, or both sides of the envelope. If you print on the front, try to print your extra message on an angle. Most word processing packages provide some way to do this or you could have a commercial printer preprint your message. Of course, you cannot obscure the

www.twrite.com

December 1, 1998

Ms. Jennifer Woods
MegaTech, Inc.
809 E. River St.
Chicago, IL 60699

Dear Ms. Woods:

Are your products ISO 9000 compliant?

TWrite, Inc. is a certified ISO 9000 consulting company. We can help you certify your products in ISO 9000 and make sure the door to the international market stays open.

You won't be disappointed with TWrite. We specialize in technical communications. In addition to ISO 9000 consulting, we've developed documentation for all kinds of companies from small software vendors to Fortune 500 companies. we have over seventeen years experience and our work won several awards from the Society for Technical Communication (STC).

If you have any questions, you can reach me at 708-778-3007 or via Email at GC@twrite.com. Check out samples of our work on our web site at www.twrite.com. I look forward to hearing from you.

With best regards,

George Conrad

George Conrad
TWrite, Inc.

Consulting

Windows Help

Technical Writing

Document Design

Online Documentation

Software/Hardware Manuals

Email:
GC@twrite.com

WWW:
twrite.com

Fax:
708.778.3008

■

TWrite, Inc.
9703 Fuller Avenue
Howard, IL 60023
708.778.3007

● Page 1 of 1

Figure11-1: Sample letterhead

recipient or return addressing information. One advantage of print-ing on the backside of the envelope is that most people turn an envelope over when they start opening it. When they do, they can see your message without any competition from the address infor-mation on the front.

Business cards

Business cards are your most important paper marketing tool. They're the easiest to carry and distribute, so you want to take full advantage of this medium. In addition to making sure you include all the information listed above, here are some tips for designing your business card.

Use both sides of the card. Rather than trying to cram all your contact information onto only one side of your business card, keep the front attractively simple and use the back for detail informa-tion. If you need even more space, use a folded business card format.

Leave space for notes. Leave space on the reverse side of your business card for you or the recipient to write notes. For example, if you attend a seminar and the speaker offers to send you addi-tional information, you can write the specifics of your request on the other side of your business card. When the speaker goes through all the business cards collected at the event, your note will remind him or her what you're requesting.

Avoid conspicuous titles. In an attempt to make an impression or simply as a matter of pride, you may be tempted to include a title for yourself on your business card. I suggest you avoid includ-ing a title such as president, CEO, or chairman on your business card. When you're a one-person business, clients may question the purpose of such a title. Actually, the only time you'll have to use a title is when you sign contracts, particularly if you are acting as an officer of your own corporation. If you feel you must have a title on your business card, you could use owner, principal, or consultant.

[FRONT]

[BACK]

Figure 11-2: Sample business card (front and back)

Brochures

Many consultants don't bother with brochures. They feel their business cards and resumes provide all the necessary paper information for a client to make a decision to hire them.

Some consultants expect too much from their brochures. They provide a stack of brochures on a table at a networking meeting and expect the brochures themselves to generate sales. If you properly position brochures, they can supplement your other informational tools, but you should not rely on them as your sole marketing tool.

Brochures fill an informational niche between your business cards and your resume. They provide more details than can fit on a business card, but are less current than a resume. That's why a typical marketing package distributed to clients includes your business card, resume, and a brochure that includes the following basic information:

What is/who is. Use this section to provide a short, one- or two-paragraph description of who you are or what your company is all about. In addition to describing your company, you may include paragraphs that describe your company philosophy or primary consulting methodology.

Services. Include a section that provides a basic description of your services. This is the section that could change the most as you add and subtract services over time.

Description of principals. Describe yourself and your professional background. Include years of experience, professional awards, professional memberships, and any professional degrees, including the schools from which you received them.

Client/project references. Include a section that describes specific experience and successes providing client solutions. This can take the form of client quotes, client testimonials, and/or project profiles.

Call to action. Give the reader a reason to call you. The easiest way to do this is to offer a free estimate for the client's project or print a coupon in your brochure that offers the first few hours of consulting for free. Make sure all the minimum contact information is in your brochure including your name, company name, address, telephone number, fax number, email address, and Web address. You may want to repeat some of this information in the header or footer on both sides of the brochure, so the reader doesn't have far to search.

Because it's more likely you will make changes in a brochure, consider using predesigned materials, especially in the early stages of your business. It is expensive to reprint custom-designed brochures. Changes are easily made in brochures printed on predesigned materials. You might even create multiple versions to address specific niches in your field.

Resumes

A resume is a familiar paper-based marketing tool. You will regularly update your resume to customize it for a particular audience and to include your most current information. For example, you will change your resume at the end of every project to update your project experience.

You will create a different resume for your business than the one you used to get a salaried job. Most people typically use a chronological format to create resumes for salaried positions. As a consultant, your skills take center stage, so organize your resume based on your skills and project experience. Brevity is just as important in your consultant resume as any other resume. Keep the resume down to one or two pages maximum.

Some consultants are uncomfortable with the term "resume." Alternative terms you can use include project description, project history, project experience, or experience. When I created my consulting resume, I didn't display any title on the document. I decided that the format and description of skills communicated its purpose.

A popular organizational method is to arrange your skills into major headings under which you describe specific projects in which you applied the skills. For example, a programmer might organize his or her skills under computer languages such as C++, Visual Basic, and Java. Under each of these categories, the programmer describes the client and the project where they used that language. You can also summarize your experience by listing the names of particular tools and/or environments. For example, a technical writer may list the word processor software packages he or she is familiar with. This type of summary is particularly useful to any agencies receiving your resume.

When you first start your consulting business, you may think you have no existing client experience to put into it. Don't forget you probably have a rich work history as an employee from which you can draw your experience. If you recategorize your employer as your "client" and reorganize your employee work experience to describe the projects you've completed and the skills you've applied, you should have plenty of material for your first consultant resume.

George Conrad / TWrite, Inc.
9703 Fuller Ave., Howard, IL 60023
▶708.778.3007 ▶GC@twrite.com ▶twrite.com   **Project Experience & Qualifications**

Online Documentation	❏ Designed online help for Xeleron's security software. ❏ Designed and coded Windows help for Riverbank Publishing's student testing application. ❏ Analyzed United Air Transport's help system for usability and delivered assessment report. ❏ Designed and coded Windows help for MegaTech's *TempTools* application. ❏ Designed and coded Windows help for London Publishing's Quantum human resources software. ❏ Wrote Windows help text and coded hyperlinks for First North Bank's *FirstWindow 2000* banking applications.
Technical Writing, Consulting, & Document Design	❏ Designed and produced award winning user documentation for London Publishing's Quanta human resources software. ❏ Wrote 237 page *Applet Developers Guide* for First North Bank's *FirstWindow 2000* Infrastructure system. ❏ Designed, wrote, and indexed 100 page User Guide and award winning 150 page Reference Guide for AmeriCorp's *Access-A-Bill* software. ❏ Wrote handbook for Arthur Anders writers describing methods for documenting COBOL programs and reading Job Control Language. ❏ Wrote standards and procedures for Query Masters Change Management System.
Document Automation	❏ Designed and coded VBA macros for Orlando's *Windows Writer's Kit*. ❏ Developed Visual Basic program for Motor One to create custom documentation on demand in Microsoft Word.

Partial Client List		
	AmeriCorp	Orlando & Associates Corporation
	Arthur Anders & Co.	Query Masters, Inc.
	First North Bank	Riverbank Publishing
	London Publishing	RR Donald & Sons
	MegaTech	United Air Transport
	Motor One, Inc.	Xeleron

Education	❏ Certificate, Technical & Professional Communications, Illinois Institute of Technology ❏ B.S., Information Science, Northeastern Illinois University
Professional memberships	❏ Senior member, Society for Technical Communication (STC) President, Chicago chapter, 1995-1996 ❏ Member, Chicago Software Association

Awards	Annual STC Technical Competition: ❏ Software Reference Guides: *Quantum for Windows User's Guide* ❏ Informational brochures: *1994 STC Independent Consultants Directory* ❏ Software Reference Guides: *Access-A-Bill Reference Manual*

Tools		
	Word for Windows	PageMaker
	RoboHelp	Adobe Acrobat
	Visual Basic	Visio

TWrite, Inc. (11/98)   www.twrite.com   708.778.3007 🖥

Figure 11-3: Sample resume

Invoices and checks

Even invoices and checks provide an opportunity to market your business. These documents may pass through many hands as they make their way through the system. It doesn't hurt to include as much contact information as possible on your checks. You may not be able to list your basic services on your checks, but you can probably include your Web and email address along with your address, phone, and fax number. Perhaps one of your vendors will notice the Web address on your check and visit your site.

Portfolios and pitch books

Depending on your industry, you may want to consider adding *portfolios* and/or *pitch books* to your bag of tricks. A portfolio provides samples of your best work. It is most appropriate for a business that delivers a fixed form product such as corporate logo, architectural drawings, or written documentation. Although these examples are primarily nontechnical and visual in nature, it can also include visual representations of more complicated work such as printed screen shots of an interface to a computer program.

What you put in your portfolio depends on your business, but wherever possible, try to provide exact duplicates or representations of the completed work. For example, if you are a graphic artist designing corporate logos, show the actual letterhead, envelope, and business card using the logo.

Pitch books are paper-based mini-presentations that allow you to step through a quick presentation with a small audience of potential clients. Pitch books are usually made up of pages in a three-ring binder, sometimes with a special attached stand that allows you to prop the binder on the client's desk. Once it's set up, you turn the pages of the binder as you go through your pitch. Because the size of the presentation is limited to standard 8½-by-11-inch pages, it is intended for informal presentations with a small audience of one or two people. If you need to present to a larger audience, prepare a projected presentation using either an overhead projector or computer projection system.

As with portfolios, the content of your pitch book varies with your business. Some pitch books make use of case studies to communicate ways in which the consultant successfully solved another client's problem. Keep in mind that a pitch book is a directed sales tool where you lead the client through the pages of the book. Whereas with a portfolio, you may allow the client to look through your samples at their own rate, picking out those items that catch their interest.

You can also provide electronic versions of portfolios and pitch books using multimedia and/or interactive presentations. For instance, you could design a portfolio or pitch book using HyperText Markup Language (HTML) or some multimedia development tool and deliver them on a diskette, a CD-ROM, or the Internet.

Marketing on the Web

> *"Experience is never limited, and it is never complete; it is an immense sensibility, a kind of huge spider-web of the finest silken threads suspended in the chamber of consciousness, and catching every air-borne particle in its tissue."*
>
> —Henry James (1843–1916), U.S. author
> *The Art of Fiction* (1884, reprinted in *Partial Portraits*, 1888)

The World Wide Web has become so ubiquitous in such a short time, it's hard to remember what we did without it. From the standpoint of a small business owner, the Web can provide a relatively inexpensive alternative to traditional mass marketing channels such as print, radio, and television advertising. With the Web you can potentially reach millions of prospects for your consulting business.

Notice I used the word "potentially." You will read many ads for Internet business products touting the "millions of people" you can reach who use the Internet. To me this is like saying because you have a telephone number, you're reaching millions of people who use the telephone. Unlike the mass marketing channels mentioned earlier (paper, television, and radio advertising), your message is not broadcast out on the Internet, but waits for someone to come knocking on your door. So, rather than working to market your entire message up front, your main goal is to publicize your Web site's address so people can find you.

This does not diminish the value of the Web as a marketing tool. The best use of the Web for an independent consultant is for an interactive brochure. Imagine having the option of simply giving someone your business card with your Web address rather than an expensively printed (and bulky) four-color paper brochure. Imagine offering capabilities beyond any paper brochure, such as downloading samples of your work or answering client questions up front. Welcome to the Internet!

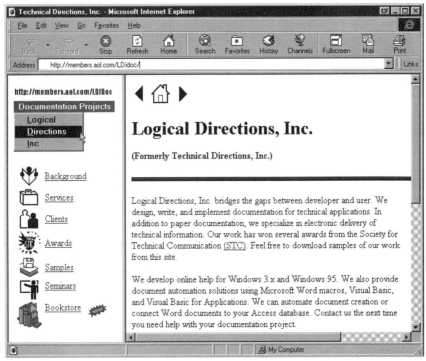

Figure 12-1: Sample Web page

What do you need to get a Web site on the Internet? This chapter refers you to several places where you can set up a free Web site under an established address. You can learn how to create the pages for your Web site yourself or hire a qualified professional to help you. There are many programs on the market for designing Web sites. Even the latest versions of the most popular word processing software can convert your information into a Web-ready document.

Inexpensive (or free) homes for your Web site

To publish your Web site you need a place to store your Web pages and an address called a Universal Resource Locator (URL) so people can access the site. The easiest way to obtain a URL is to piggyback on an established Web site provided by your current Internet Service Provider (ISP) or some other Internet company. When you're ready to establish your own unique presence on the Web, your ISP can usually handle the paperwork to register your URL.

The host server Web site maintains the hardware, software, and phone lines necessary to operate as a server on the Internet. They provide disk storage space and software. They also provide consulting services (usually for a fee) so individuals and businesses like yours can operate a Web site without having to maintain your own equipment. There are many choices of inexpensive and even free host server sites where you can publish your Web site.'

Using space on your current Internet provider's system

Chances are, you already use an ISP or information service such as CompuServe or America Online to access the Internet. Many ISPs offer a limited amount of space on their server for you to host your Web site.

In addition to the space included with your subscription, most ISPs also offer optional space and features for an additional fee. Optional features include things like site monitoring and logging that informs you about the traffic going through your site and advanced programming capability such as the Common Gateway Interface (CGI) that lets you provide a more interactive Web site.

Free host sites

There are several Internet sites that provide free space to anyone who wants to set up a Web site. Often called communities, these master Web sites provide many megabytes of free space and publishing tools. What's the catch? Generally, these sites get their revenue from advertisers, so while someone is viewing your site, they may see an advertisement for some unrelated product or service. These sites get their advertising dollars because they attract a lot of browsers, so this can increase traffic to your site.

Keep in mind that even though these sites provide free hosting services, they still have rules and restrictions as to what you can put on their site. Although rules vary from site to site, here are some common restrictions:

- You cannot use any copyrighted material without the express permission of the author or owner.
- You cannot create pages that promote illegal activity.
- You cannot create pages that defame, abuse, or threaten others.
- Most sites have restrictions on material that is grossly offensive to their online community. This includes clear expressions of bigotry, racism, or hatred; images that exploit children under 18 years of age; and pornography.
- Usually, you may not sell advertising space for other businesses on your page (for example, paid advertising banners). Sometimes you can participate in banner exchange programs that help promote your site by mentioning the host site.
- You cannot use your free storage space to save and "park" files and data for you to download at a later date. In other words, these sites don't want you using their storage space as an extension of your computer's disk drive.

Here is a list of several popular free host sites:

GeoCities (www.geocities.com) offers 11 megabytes of storage space on a high-traffic site organized around a community theme. However, they have strict guidelines that prohibit commercial activity on their free Web sites and they discourage links from one of their free sites to a commercial or any other site outside GeoCities. Despite this, if you carefully organize your site as an information provider or newsletter, you can take advantage of what GeoCities has to offer.

If you want a more formal business presence on GeoCities and you are willing to pay a monthly fee, they offer GeoShops. For an additional monthly fee, GeoShops offers a range of added features including an online store, multiple topic search categories, additional server storage space, unlimited email aliases, a library of utilities and programming modules, and credit card processing. They'll also help you register your own URL.

Angelfire Communications (www.angelfire.com) provides 5 megabytes of free storage space and a set of utilities to build your home pages. You can advertise your business on your page, run banner link exchange programs, create a guest book, choose from a variety of graphics, and add sound files. They also use the *Who Where?* directory of email addresses, personal home pages, telephone listings, business URLs, and communication tools so browsers can find you.

XOOM (www.xoom.com) provides unlimited storage space. They also provide free software to build your Web page without knowing HTML and a free email account. Using this site you can participate in chats, message boards, and communities.

Tripod (www.tripod.com) provides 11 megabytes of free storage space. Tripod organizes member Web pages into common themes, topics, or interests called "Pods." Tripod members can participate in as many Pods as they like. As a member of a Pod (or Pods), you can participate in all Pod events, including chat and conferencing (message boards). If you have a home page that is related to the Pod topic, you can submit it for inclusion on the Pod publisher's list. Pods are built and maintained by volunteer "Poderators" who keep the Pod focused on its theme or topic, help manage chats, and write and distribute a Pod newsletter to keep members informed of Pod events. Tripod also offers a premium membership service for an additional monthly fee. The premium membership includes an email forwarding address, personal chat area, 22 megabytes of storage space, a premium membership newsletter, special image library providing images for your Web page, and a discount on Tripod apparel.

Webspawner (www.Webspawner.com) provides one free page, with up to 25 kilobytes of space. For a monthly fee, you can add additional space and services. Although the free Web page service is limited to one page, Webspawner has a simple setup process without HTML that only requires you to fill out an online form. Webspawner will also register your Web page with over 120 search engines, Web page listings, and indexes for a one-time fee. Considering the limited size of the free area in Webspawner, you may want to consider setting up a more robust site on one of the other free host sites and use your Webspawner Web site to link to your main site.

Creating Your Own Internet Identity

The problem with using free host sites or space on your ISP's system is that you will probably end up with a long and hard-to-remember URL. The part of the URL before ".com" is called the domain name. There is a relatively inexpensive way in which you can create your own unique domain name and simplify your Web site address to www.*your-name*.com by using an Internet registration system like www.namesecure.com.

NameSecure.com will register your domain name, forward visitors to the actual location of your Web site, and forward email addressed as *your-name@your-name*.com to wherever your actual email is received. The cost of this service is covered by an initial registration fee (currently $70) and a yearly maintenance fee (currently $24.95) paid to NameSecure.

The initial registration fee covers the cost to register your domain name with InterNic, the agency resonsible for maintaining all the Internet domain names. After your initial two year registration, there is a modest yearly fee (currently $35) paid to InterNic to maintain your domain name registration.

So, as of this writing, after the first two years of operation, your yearly maintenance cost for the NameSecure service is just $59.95. The beauty of this service is the actual location of your Web pages can be anywhere—on a free Web host site, on your ISP's site, or anywhere else. Even if you move your Web site, visitors can still find you because the NameSecure service will forward them to your new location once you let NameSecure know where it's located.

Content: What to put on your Web site

A Web site for your business serves as your electronic brochure. Although it may be similar in nature to its paper counterpart, a Web site can provide information to potential clients in a way that no paper brochure can. The Web lets you provide up-to-date details about your business including supplemental documents that Web viewers can download as desired.

There are many ways to design a Web page. There are entire sections of major bookstores devoted to Web design, so it's beyond the scope of this book to teach optimum Web design. Also, many Web design software packages provide templates that can get you started. Included here are some general categories of information that you should consider for your Web site.

Background page

This type of information is often also called "Who we are" or "About us." The background page of your Web site serves as a brief resume of you and your company. Information you can put on this page includes your company's goals, services, and type of clients you've served. This would also be a good place to put a short professional biography about yourself.

Services page

If applicable, divide your services into service categories and include a general description of each service. Make sure you focus on the benefits of each service to your clients. Because of the unique nature of most consulting projects, consider carefully whether you want to include pricing for your services.

Samples page

As appropriate to your type of business, try to provide samples of your work that potential clients can view or download from your Web site. For example, as a technical communicator, I provide sections of publications I've worked on, reflecting my best work. A programmer consultant may provide a small demo program that potential clients can download. Another good use for this page is to provide a downloadable copy of your resume.

If you provide files to download, what format should you use? For standard documents you want to use a medium common to most computer users. This is difficult in a computer environment that includes Microsoft/Intel, Macintosh, Unix, and other types of computer users. Here are some suggestions for common document formats recognized by all the major word processing applications and operating systems:

ASCII text. Documents written with the American Standard Code for Information Interchange (ASCII) use a standard format that almost any word processing program or text editor on any type of operating system can open. Most word processors as well as simple text editors like Microsoft Notepad can write files in ASCII format. The disadvantage with this format is that you cannot use font styles and formatting like bold and italics.

RTF documents. Rich Text Format (RTF) is a Microsoft standard document format that most major word processing programs can read and write. Unlike ASCII text, it lets you use font styles and formatting.

Adobe Acrobat files. Adobe Systems created the Acrobat format to preserve the original layout of documents, including fonts, images, tables, and multicolumn text. People who view Acrobat files can find information by viewing a table of contents and thumbnail pictures of each page, or searching the entire text of the document. Anyone who wants to view an Acrobat file can download a free copy of the reader program from Adobe at www.adobe.com and the major browser software programs include Acrobat reader software. Adobe provides readers for almost every computer platform including Microsoft Windows, Macintosh, and Unix. To create Acrobat files you must purchase the Adobe Acrobat authoring software. The authoring software works with applications like Microsoft Word and Excel to publish Acrobat files directly from those applications.

Awards page

If your work has won any awards, create a page describing your accomplishments. If possible, you can also provide examples of the award-winning work for Web viewers to download.

Associated products

Another important use of your Web page is to market any associated products you've developed or other vendors products you're reselling. Some ideas include books, reports, seminars, and software programs you've developed related to your business. You can also become a reseller for vendors of related products. For example, if you are a programmer consultant you might resell software related to your work.

One easy reseller business anyone can set up is book sales. The best example of this is the Amazon Associate's program provided by Amazon.com. By following a few rules, anyone can set up an Amazon "bookstore" with links to Amazon's Web site. As an Amazon Associate, you can earn from 5 to 15 percent on any book a person purchases by passing through your Web site. Since Amazon sells books about any subject, it's easy to compile a list of books related to your field. Amazon encourages its associates to provide personal commentaries on books they've selected. One simple way to create a list of books for your Web site is to simply look at the business and professional books on your own bookshelf. If you compile a good list supplemented with your commentary and updated often, you provide another reason for people to revisit your site.

Associated links

Another way to add value to your Web site is to compile a list of related Web sites. Companies such as Yahoo, Alta Vista, and Lycos built their businesses on helping people find relevant Web sites on the Internet. You can provide a similar service, albeit on a much smaller scale, by maintaining an organized list of related links.

Industry news and tips

You can turn your Web site into a newsletter by providing news and/or tips about your industry. If you decide to go this route, you must update this page often so the information doesn't get stale.

Getting people to your Web site

Creating and publishing your Web site is only the beginning. All that hard work will go to waste if no one can find your Web site without knowing the exact URL. An important part of your Web strategy is to promote your site. Fortunately, the Web provides several low cost ways to do this.

Search engines

The best way to get the word out on your Web site is to register it with as many search engines as possible. Search engines like Yahoo, AltaVista, Excite, Lycos, and InfoSeek, let browsers find Web sites based on search criteria they specify. You want to make sure a search of Web sites relevant to your business includes a link to your Web site. Here are some tips for working with search engines.

Register your Web site. You can register your Web site with the main search engines in two ways. You can either manually submit your registration to each search engine or you can use one of several registration services to do the job for you. Several registration services such as Submit It!, PostMaster, and Add It! let you enter basic information about your site once and then submit this information to the search engines you select. Some registration services do this for free while others charge a fee. The Recommended Resources section of this book provides a list of search engines and registration services. Keep in mind that most search engines have a waiting period before they list a page, ranging from a few minutes to a few weeks. Whether you register once with a registration service or multiple times with the different search engines, be prepared to provide some basic information about your site. Although the required registration information varies with different search engines and registration services, here is a list of common information most require:

- Your Web site's URL.
- A list of keywords that describe your Web site.
- A 35-to-50-word description of your Web site.
- The name, email address, and phone number of a contact person.

Make your Web site "search-engine friendly." In addition to the basic information you submit to a search engine or registration service when you register your page, search engines compile information, such as keywords and abstracts, from the text information and HTML tags contained in the site's individual Web pages. They do this using special software called "spiders." You enhance the chances that a browser will find your site and that the search engine will provide meaningful information by imbedding specific information in your Web site.

Here are some design tips to make your Web site search-engine friendly:

- Avoid symbols in your URLs because many search engines do not recognize them.

- The search engines draw much of their information from the home page of your site. This is usually the first page a browser sees when they visit your site. Don't design a home page that contains only graphics. Besides taking longer to download, graphically intensive home pages don't provide enough text for a search engine to use. So, make sure you have text on your home page.

- Place a summary paragraph at the top of each page describing page contents. Include keywords that browsers are likely to use in a search for your site and limit the summary to around 250 words or less.

- Keep in mind that each search engine has different methods of deciding what criteria is best for their engines. Therefore, it is a good idea to learn as much as you can about specific engines so that you can target them.

- Refrain from registering your site with a search engine more than once. If you do this with some search engines they lower your ranking in any search results list.

- Place descriptive keywords between the <TITLE> HTML tags on each page of your Web site.

- Use <META> HTML tags to provide additional description and keywords for search engines. For example, the <META> HTML code for a Web page description is:

<META Name = "description" content = "Your page description">

For keywords, the HTML code is:

<META Name = "keywords" content = "Keyword1, Keyword2, etc">

- Be creative when selecting keywords. Keep in mind not everyone thinks of the same words you do, especially when you consider an international audience. For example, while we call a certain type of store a "drug store," the British call them "chemists." For this reason, you should try to include a wide range of keywords relevant to your site. You should even consider including commonly misspelled words because many people are not aware of the correct spelling. Include misspelled words only in hidden Web page information like <META> tags and not in any text displayed to the browser.
- Use the <ALT> HTML tag to describe your graphics. Since search engines cannot read graphics, this provides a text description the search engine can use.

Banner ads

Banner exchange services display banners for members of the network on member Web sites. Sometimes a portion of the banner space is sold to sponsors, which allows the exchange site to offer this service for free.

Here is a list of some banner exchange Web sites:

- LinkExchange (http://www.linkexchange.com)
- Bannerswap (http://www.bannerswap.com)
- LinkTrader (http://www.linktrader.com)

Yellow pages

Sites that offer Internet Yellow Pages are similar to paper Yellow Pages. They help browsers searching for a specific topic find

Web pages pertaining to that subject. Two sites that operate Internet Yellow Pages are AT&T Toll-Free Internet Pages (www.att.net/dir800/) and GTE Superpages (www.yp.gte.net/).

Classified ads

Another way to publicize your Web site is to list it on Internet classified Web sites. Most of these sites offer some sort of free ad service. Usually for additional fees, you can display more lines of text or even one Web page. Here is a list of sites that offer Internet classified ads:

- 1 Mall (www.1mall.com/)
- American Business Classified (www.abcads.com/)
- American Internet Classifieds (www.bestads.com/)
- E-Mart (www.e-mart.co.uk/)
- EPages Internet Classifieds (www.ep.com/)
- Internet www/Buy 'n' Sell (www.netbistro.com/)
- Progressive Possibilities (www.callamer.com/macronet/index/classify/)
- WWW Classifieds (www.fy.com/)

Reciprocal links

A simple way to increase your Web site's exposure is to get listed in the associated links page of other Web sites. You can do this informally by contacting other complementary businesses and offering to provide a link to their Web site in exchange for a reciprocal link on your Web site.

The Web site Missing Link (http://www.igoldrush.com/missing/) provides a database of Web sites who exchange links with other Web sites. You can search the database for appropriate sites with which you can exchange links and list your own site in the database. When you list your own site, you can specify any restrictions on who can exchange links with you. For instance, you may restrict link exchanges to competing companies in your industry.

Marketing to Agencies

*"O world, world! thus is the poor agent despised.
O traitors and bawds, how earnestly are you
set a-work, and how ill requited! Why should
our endeavor be so loved, and the performance
so loathed?"*

—William Shakespeare (1564–1616), English dramatist, poet.
Pandarus, in *Troilus and Cressida*, act 5, scene 10, Quarto ed.

As described earlier, an agency is a company that places contract employees on assignments with their clients. Agencies are also called consulting firms, job shops, and brokers. Whatever the name, they typically will play a part in your marketing plan, particularly in the early years of your business.

From a marketing standpoint, independent consultants act as wholesalers to agencies. Some consultants work exclusively for agencies. By leaving the marketing to the agency and avoiding the time and effort required to acquire their own direct clients, they can concentrate exclusively on their work. Other consultants work through agencies during the early years of their business while they develop their own separate, direct clients. As they build up their own client base, these consultants start to phase out the agencies because most agencies cannot offer the same "retail" rate consultants get from their own clients.

Advantages of using agencies

There are several advantages when you market to agencies, including the following.

You can often find work quickly. Particularly in the early years of your consulting business, agencies can provide work quickly while you establish yourself.

They buffer you from the client. Most agency contracts don't withhold payment to you if the client does not pay them. Theoretically, the agency "guarantees" that you get paid even if the client doesn't pay them. Most agencies must carry proper business liability and workers compensation insurance. Some even carry errors and omissions insurance to cover mistakes in your work. This buffers you somewhat from client litigation. Finally, if there is a personality conflict between you and the client, the agency can step in and mitigate the situation.

They act as your "salesperson." Most agencies maintain a staff of salespeople that market the agency's services on a full-time basis. An agency is only as good as the people it hires or subcontracts. When the agency sells its services, it's also selling yours.

They may provide benefits. Some agencies provide limited benefits such as health insurance or 401(k) retirement plans if you work for them as a W-2 contractor (temporary employee).

Some clients may work only with agencies. Some clients will only subcontract work out to an agency. These clients feel this protects them from an IRS audit that could redefine the subcontractors as their employees, forcing them to pay the IRS employee withholding taxes. If you really want to do work for a particular client with this restriction, you may have to do it through an agency.

Disadvantages of using agencies

Be aware of the following disadvantages of marketing to agencies.

You trade revenue to cover the agency's overhead. An agency marks up your rate anywhere from 20 to 100 percent to cover their overhead and profit. If the agency is paying you $50 an hour, they may charge the client as much as $100.

Judging whether the agency's markup is "fair" is a subjective exercise. Some agencies invest literally hundreds of person hours marketing to a client before the client buys the agency's services. As an independent consultant, it's hard to duplicate this kind of intense marketing effort yourself. Other agencies are notorious for getting contracts based on low price and haranguing their subcontractors into taking a lower rate, hoping the difference will cover their overhead.

You cannot market to the agency's client for a period of time. Most agency contracts include a noncompete clause. This clause prevents you from directly soliciting business from the client to whom you're providing services through the agency, for a specific period of time. The blackout period ranges anywhere from six months to two years, but the average is one year. The agency feels it needs this clause because it knows that with your low overhead, you can always undercut their rate if you directly market to their client. They feel the clause is justified because it allows them time to recoup their marketing expenses.

You cannot control what the agency tells the client about you. Most agencies operate professionally and ethically. I have heard stories about agencies, desperate to sell to a particular client, inflating, distorting, or outright lying about a consultant's experience or skills without his or her knowledge. If this happens, you could actually show up for work and discover the client expects you to perform some service that is completely outside the scope of your abilities. Obviously, this puts you in a very difficult position with the client.

Typically, you can avoid this when you meet with the client during the negotiation stages, during which you clearly outline your abilities to the client and investigate their needs. Immediately break off any further activity with any agency that asks you to exaggerate, obscure, or lie about your experience or skills.

Where to find agencies

To take advantage of them, you need to build a large list of agencies. Some agencies may subcontract to consultants in your field only once or twice a year on average, so you need to accumulate the names of many agencies to increase the odds of being called. Once you build your list, you can mass mail your resume to the agencies so you can get into their database of contractors.

The Recommended Resources section of this book includes a short list of agencies. Here are some other places to look for agencies.

Newspapers. Check the classified ads of your local paper, looking under the appropriate category for your field. Agencies with work constantly advertise. Even if an agency advertises for permanent agency employees, they may be open to hiring you as a contractor in the future.

Trade papers. Sometimes trade papers do profiles of an agency or publish a list of agencies for a particular field. Agency experts often write articles for trade papers. Agencies also place ads in industry trade papers.

Contractor publications. There are publications targeted to contractors that publish articles, agency ads, and listings of current contracts. Two such publications are *PD News* and *C.E. Weekly. PD News* publishes an annual *Directory of Technical Service Firms* that lists about 800 agencies. In addition to weekly delivery, a subscription to *PD News* includes agency mailing labels and a membership in the National Association for the Self-Employed (NASE). *C.E. Weekly's* subscription includes the annual *Directory of Contract Service Firms,* which lists about 1,000 agencies. There is more information about both these publications in the Recommended Resources section of this book.

Both these publications offer a resume mailing service. For a small fee, they will mail your resume to all the agencies on their list. Keep in mind that if you use this service, they send your resume to agencies all over the country, possibly even the world. Even if you make it clear in your resume that you only want projects in your area, you may receive calls from agencies all over the place. Other agencies that operate in areas with a shortage of qualified consultants may still call you in a desperate effort to fill a contract in their area, hoping they can convince you to travel.

Word-of-mouth. When searching for agencies, don't forget to consult your usual network. Ask friends and colleagues about any agencies they have either hired or worked for. While most fellow independent consultants will understandably be reticent about sharing their client list with you, most have no problem sharing the list of agencies for whom they've contracted. By soliciting opinions from other independent consultants, you can find out which agencies pay the best and provide the fairest contracts.

Yellow Pages. You also can supplement your list of agencies by consulting the telephone Yellow Pages. Usually, there is no general "consultants" listing there, so you will probably have to look for agencies as subclassifications under general headings. Also, you may need to look under several related subjects to find agencies that market your kind of skills. For example, to find agencies that handle technical writers, I would first look under "Writers." But, I know that many computer consulting agencies handle technical writers, so I would also look under the subject "Computers—System Designers and Consultants."

It may be more difficult to separate agencies advertising in the Yellow Pages that subcontract work from small-shop companies that do all the work themselves. But even other independent consultants advertising in the Yellow Pages may need a subcontractor in the future, so it can't hurt to include most of the companies you find in the Yellow Pages.

Internet. The Internet is an exceptional source for finding agencies. You can use the various search engines to find agencies or you can connect to one of many job boards. As of this writing, one popular job board designed for computer independent consultants is the Data Processing Independent Consultants Exchange (DICE) at www.dice.com. DICE includes a company directory consisting of agencies who participate on the DICE Web page. You can search for agencies by name, region, or type of work.

Job fairs. Many industries promote periodic job fairs sponsored by agencies, recruiters, and other companies. Since agencies heavily attend these events, job fairs provide an excellent opportunity to meet face-to-face with many agencies in one place. In addition to personally distributing your resume, job fairs usually provide a list of all the companies (including agencies) that exhibit at the fair.

You can use this information to build your agency list and send your resume to any agencies you did not talk to at the fair.

When I first started my consulting business, I attended a job fair for people in the computer software field. In addition to distributing my resume to agencies exhibiting booths at the fair, I obtained a free list of other agencies associated with the fair. I used that list to send out more than 50 resumes and received my first contract only weeks after that mailing.

Tips on marketing to agencies

Here are some general tips to keep in mind while you're building your agency marketing plan.

Mass mail your resume to agencies

Particularly in the first year of your business, agencies may provide a large portion of your business. The quickest way to get the word out is to mass mail your resume with a cover letter to as many agencies as you can find. Try to build a list of 50 to 100 agencies.

Agencies don't mind receiving unsolicited mail. Their business depends on accumulating a large database of consultants, so if you have skills they sell, they will put your resume into their database. It may be a while before they call you with a potential project, but when the opportunity arises, they will call.

Set your agency discount rate ahead of time

Decide ahead of time what you will quote agencies when they ask you about your rate. When an agency calls you about a potential project, they typically avoid telling you what the contract will pay and turn the question around by asking you what you charge. Some agencies do this because at that point, they aren't sure what the client is willing to pay. Or they may have already quoted the client their price and they are trying to get as large a markup as they can from your rate. Don't forget that agencies make their money by charging the client as much as they can and paying you as little as they can. Few agencies will reveal their standard markup.

Rather than stumbling around trying to get the agency to reveal the maximum rate they are willing to pay for a project, offer the agency a standard discount from the rate you charge your direct clients. As discussed in Chapter 5, consider this your "wholesale" rate and the rate you charge your direct clients your "retail" or standard rate. See Chapter 5 for more information on setting your rate structure.

Sell your advantages, not your price

The good news about independent consulting is that it's relatively easy to start a business. The bad news is, because it's so easy to get into independent consulting, many inexperienced and downright unqualified people enter the field. Many of these people try to get hired by offering the lowest possible rate. Sometimes these people do this because they know they lack key skills and figure they are "discounting" their rate to compensate for this. Others may be very good at what they do but either lack the confidence to charge what they're worth or neglect to properly research rates for their field. In either case, these consultants probably are losing money on their business and don't even know it! You never want to make your "low rate" your main selling point when marketing to agencies.

If an agency questions what you are charging them, describe your value-added attributes. Here are some examples.

Awards. Describe any industry awards you've received for related work. This demonstrates recognition for your work from your peers and differentiates you from other consultants.

Special training. If you completed a special seminar, certificate program, or degree specific to your field, describe this as a selling point for the agency. It reinforces to their clients that the agency selects highly trained, credentialed professionals.

Client industry experience. If you have performed the exact service for another client in the same industry as the agency's client, this enhances your qualifications for the project.

Skill with a special tool. If you are certified by a product vendor or can demonstrate you are an expert at a tool that has a limited number of experts, this helps justify your rate.

Agency savings on payroll taxes. If the agency pays you as a corporation or on a 1099 basis, the agency does not have to pay

W-2 employer payroll taxes since they are not declaring you as their temporary employee. These savings can help them fund the rate you are charging.

Make it easy for the agency to use your resume

Typically, an agency takes your resume and then reformats it to their own style before submitting it to their client. When they do this they highlight your relevant skills and remove your name so the client cannot drop the agency and call you directly. There is nothing unusual about this procedure, provided the agency does not falsify anything on your resume.

You can make the agency's job easier by providing both paper and electronic copies of your resume. If the agency has a hot project, they will request you fax your resume to them. You can also offer to send them an electronic copy by email or you can make it available for download from your Web site. I suggest you create a copy of your resume using Rich Text Format (RTF) specifically for this purpose. All the major word processing programs provide the option of generating and reading documents in RTF. This format lets you use all the standard word processing features (bold, italic, variable fonts, etc.) while providing a common format the agency can read and edit on its own system.

Inform agencies about any potential noncompete conflicts

Before you and an agency get too excited about working with a potential client, make sure you double-check that you are not restricted from working with that client. If another agency hired you to work for that same client in the past, even if it was for a different department, your previous agreement may restrict you from working for that client under a new agency.

When you sign a contract with an agency, it usually includes a noncompete clause that restricts you from working for the client either directly or under someone else for a certain period of time, usually for a year. If a new agency wants you to work for the same client and the noncompete is still in effect, you must inform the agency and disqualify yourself from consideration until the noncompete clause expires, or request permission from the other agency.

Agencies to avoid

I've had good experiences with the agencies I've worked with, although there are some bad apples. Avoid any agencies that do the following.

They always try to negotiate down your rate. As mentioned earlier, some agencies try to get their foot in a client's door by selling their services on price alone. When they do this, they leave little room for negotiation with you, the consultant. Turn down any agency that offers you a rate that insults your intelligence. If you did your homework and established an intelligent rate for agencies, you don't need to waste time with agencies that lowball you on rates.

They ask you to lie or exaggerate your skills or experience. Based on your own experience or information you receive from a good source, avoid any agency with a reputation for distorting information about a contractor's skill or experience. The agency may reveal this tendency during your negotiations with them. For example, your resume may mention some light experience you received in one type of work while delivering another service. An unscrupulous agency may try to convince you to let them promote you as an "expert" in that area.

They don't understand what you do. If you talk with an agency salesperson or recruiter who asks you to define basic terms or acronyms they find in your resume, it either means they are testing you or their firm is venturing into a new field it doesn't understand. When you start talking to new agencies, ask them about their experience marketing in the industry from which you draw your experience. Ask them to send you a copy of their standard marketing materials. If an agency specializes in providing health care professionals, it may not understand how to market computer programmers.

They ask you for strategic or proprietary information. Although it's fair and even to your advantage for agencies to ask you to identify clients and the type of work you've done, it's not appropriate for agencies to pump you for proprietary information. Depending on the type of nondisclosure agreements you may have signed with other clients and agencies, it may even be illegal for you to provide this information.

They submit your resume without your permission. Some agencies try to impress a client with the depth of their contractor base by submitting resumes of consultants before checking the consultant's availability. Other agencies play a game of "bait and switch" with clients, presenting the resume of their best consultants to get the client's attention. If the client requests one of those individuals, the agency may call the consultant and see if he or she is available without telling the consultant that they've been preselected. Or, more likely, they inform the client that the consultant had to take another assignment, but the agency can offer someone who's "just as good." It may be a long time before you discover that an agency engages in this type of practice, but if word gets back to you that an agency submitted your resume without your permission, scratch that agency off your list.

There is another practical reason why you don't want agencies submitting your resume without your permission. It's possible that another agency plans to submit your resume to the same client. The odds are that the two agencies will quote different rates to the client for the same resource, namely, you. At the very least, this will confuse the client. By requiring your permission and asking some questions about the client, you can screen the agency project to see if it matches any other projects for which you've allowed an agency to submit your resume.

They expect you to continue working without a contract. As a general rule, you should not start working on a project unless you have a signed contract. This applies to work done for agencies as well as direct clients. To accommodate a client's deadline, you may occasionally agree to start working on a project while you and the agency nail down the details of a contract. Even in this situation, the agency should give you a review copy of their standard contract. If you start working at a client without seeing the agency contract, you risk an embarrassing situation for you and the agency if you have to pull out of the project because you cannot come to terms later on.

The agency cycle

There is a typical cycle of events when dealing with any agency: initial screening, project negotiation, and delivery.

Initial screening phase

During this phase, the agency satisfies itself that you are the type of person with whom it can continue working.

First contact. The agency may contact you in response to your mailing or after getting your name from some other source. If the agency does not have any work at present, it is screening you for its database. If there is an immediate project, the agency will combine the initial screening with the project negotiation phase. In either case, during this step, the agency will ask you about your career experience and current availability.

Have your resume in front of you and practice reciting the highlights of your background. Ask the agency how long it has been marketing professionals in your field.

Preliminary rate disclosure. If the agency likes what it's heard up to this point, you will be asked to quote your hourly rate. This is your chance to find out if the agency is willing to pay it. If you did your homework and researched your rate properly, you're prepared for this question.

If the agency does not have a specific project in mind for you, it may simply accept your quoted rate without telling you that it is higher than it is willing to pay. In this case, the agency figures it can negotiate you down when an actual project is on the table. Or it will tell you on the spot the rate you quoted is too high. If the agency has a particular project in mind when it calls you, it may have already quoted the client the rate, leaving limited room for negotiation.

If an agency expresses concern that your rate is too high and you don't want to lower your rate, try to differentiate yourself from the average consultant it usually places. Demonstrate the rationale behind your rate by citing your years of experience, awards you've won, and unique skills. Most agencies spend the majority of their time trying to fill skills consulting type projects. Suggest to the agency that it save you for more advanced projects such as project management or expert-advice consulting.

Exchange of information. If the agency feels it can handle your rate and wants to add you to its database, it will request that you send an updated resume. At this point, you should also ask the agency to send you its standard marketing materials.

Ask the agency in what format you should send your resume. You can fax it or attach an electronic version to an email message. If you discover through your discussions that the agency specializes in a particular segment of your field, you can rearrange your resume to highlight skills that apply to that particular specialty. When you talk to the agency, get essential contact information such as name, address, phone, email, and so forth. Also, ask the agency to provide you with a standard version of its contract. This lets you review the agency contract before you start negotiating for a particular client project.

Agency interview. In addition to requesting your resume, the best agencies always request to meet with you before marketing you to a client. As part of the initial screening process, an agency may request to meet with you even if there is no current project. During the interview, the agency primarily wants to see how well you present yourself. The agency may also ask you to fill out a standard form so it can easily enter your skills in its database. The agency interview also gives you a chance to see the agency's office and assess its professionalism.

As with any interview, always dress professionally. If you have any samples of your work, this is the time to show them to the agency. Your main goal is to communicate confidence in your skills and to build a good partnership with the agency.

Project negotiation phase. During this phase of the agency cycle, the agency contacts you to satisfy a specific client project request.

Project screening. When the agency tries to fill a client request to outsource a project with subcontractors, it searches its database of consultants and calls those who seem to match the client's criteria. The skill the agency exercises in this search varies from company to company. Some understand the client's requirements and are very good at narrowing the search to a relevant set of candidates.

Others simply call everyone whose resume even remotely mentions similar work. Because you can't count on the agency to always match you with an appropriate project, this is also your chance to screen the project to match your current circumstances.

There are three basic pieces of information you need to decide if you will take on the project: type of work, rate, and location. First, you need to make sure the project is suitable for your skills and the work interests you. Second, you need to find out what rate the agency will pay for the project to see if it meets your minimum requirements. Finally, you need to find out where the client is located and whether you will be working onsite or at your home office. If the project is out of town and you don't want to travel that far, you should turn the project down. If the project requires extensive driving, you may want to ask for a higher rate to cover the time and cost of daily commuting.

Client interview. If the project matches your basic criteria and you are available to do the project, the agency will ask your permission to submit your resume to the client. If the client expresses interest, the agency will arrange a formal interview between you and the client. An agency representative will also attend the interview to introduce you to the client.

Remember during the interview you and the agency are both comarketing your skills to the client. To the client, you represent the agency and not yourself. As veteran consultant and publisher Christopher Juillet put it, "You must consider yourself part of the agency's team. Nothing upsets an agency more than a 'rogue' consultant."

Agency offer. If the client likes you, the agency will offer you a contract. If you agree to take on the project, the agency will send you a written contract that identifies the scope of your work and the rate you negotiated.

Review the agency's contract carefully. If you requested a standard contract during the initial screening phase, you can check the project contract against it. If the contract is long and complicated, you may want an attorney to examine it. Your decision to incur attorney's fees may depend on the value of the contract. A good rule of thumb is to use an attorney if the contract is worth $10,000 or more. Despite the agency's assertion that it "will not change the contract" most agencies will negotiate changes when they are faced with a client who has already signed off on a consultant and is anxious to get started. See Chapter 16 for more information on contracts.

Delivery phase

After you and the agency come to terms and sign a contract, you will start delivering the contracted services to the client.

Work for client. Typically, an agency representative will show up on your first day with the client to make sure things are off to a good start. If the agency is providing a large number of consultants to the client, you may report to an agency project manager. Many agencies, however, do not actively manage their consultants, so you will either manage yourself or report to a client manager.

Make sure you understand the agency's and the client's procedures for reporting your hours and progress on the project.

Project conclusion. When the project reaches its contractual completion date, it either terminates or the client asks to extend it. If the contract terminates, you will bid farewell to the client and plan your next project. If the agency has another contract available, you will repeat the project negotiation phase. The client often will extend the contract to either complete the work or to start another related project. This is quite common in computer programming projects because they are hard to schedule accurately.

If the client and the agency requests to extend your contract, review the terms of your agreement regarding extensions. You may want to use the request for an extension as an opportunity to renegotiate portions of the agreement. Before you leave a project, ask both the client and the agency if you can use them as references for future projects. If appropriate for your field, you may also want to request permission to use samples from the project for your portfolio.

Creating a Marketing Plan 14

"In preparing for battle I have always found that plans are useless, but planning is indispensable."

—Dwight D. Eisenhower (1890–1969)
quoted by Richard Nixon in *Six Crises*, "Krushchev" (1962)

The core of your consulting business is your marketing plan. Creating a marketing plan is not a one-time exercise. You will continue to review and tweak your marketing plan while you deliver your services.

To make the task a little easier, I developed a one-page form for organizing your marketing plan that is included in the Sample Worksheets section of this book. The form answers the three most important questions about your marketing plan:

• What methods will I use?

• When do I use them?

• How much will it cost me?

Vertically, the form divides several marketing methods discussed earlier in this book into Passive and Active categories. Horizontally, it is divided into four major sections: Method, Implementation, Cost, and Timing (by month).

Method. The method column of the form lists several of the methods discussed in this book and divides them into passive and active methods. The passive methods include directory listings, advertising, mass mail, and publicity. The active methods include networking, cold calling, public speaking, and seminars. You can replace or augment any of these with your own methods. The blank version of the form in the Sample Worksheets section of the book includes blank sections for this.

Implementation. Under implementation, for each method specify how you will carry out the method. See the sample marketing plan shown in the figure. Often, you will have more than one implementation for a method. For example, in figure 14-1, this consultant will list his business in two directories: the main Society for Technical Communication (STC) *Membership Directory* and the local STC chapter's *Directory of Independent Consultants.*

Cost. Opposite each method implementation, enter the estimated cost to carry out the implementation. Sometimes several marketing items are covered by one expense. For example, in the figure opposite the networking method, this consultant will attend an STC conference at a cost of $1,000. However, he will do more than network at this conference. He will also do public speaking by participating in a panel discussion and he'll present a seminar.

Timing. I've divided the timing side of the form into columns for each month of the year. To signify when an event for a particular implementation of a marketing method is to occur, enter the day under the appropriate month. For example, in the figure, this consultant decided to make 20 cold calls on the fifteenth of every month.

*There's an old saying: "plan your work and work your plan." But, as a one person consulting business you have to **plan** and **work** at the same time.*

Most consulting experts and veteran consultants feel that you should spend 20 percent of your time marketing. This is difficult when you have one or more projects that always demand your time. However, by leveraging passive marketing techniques that

Marketing plan for 1999

Method	Implementation	Cost	Jan	Feb	Mar	Apr	May	Jun	Jul	Aug	Sep	Oct	Nov	Dec
Passive														
Directory Listings	STC chapter Directory of Independent Consultants	$60								01				
	STC Memberhsip Directory	$95											01	
Advertising	Advertise in Chicago Computer Guide	$450	01											
Mass Mail	Mail 10 brochures per week	$172	wkly	wkly	wkly	wkly	wkly	wkly	wkly	wkly	wkly	wkly	wkly	wkly
Publicity	Support public radio	$300			15									
Active														
Networking	Attend STC chapter meetings	$270	20	16	25	22	20	16			25	22	18	
	Attend STC conference	$1,000					16-19							
Cold Calling	Make 20 cold calls per month	$0	15	15	15	15	15	15	15	15	15	15	15	15
Public speaking	Participate in panel discussion at STC Conference	$0					18							
Seminars	Conduct seminar at STC Conference	$0					20							
	Total Cost:	$2,347												

Figure 14-1: Sample marketing plan

do some of the marketing work for you, and reserving some time to network and market to new prospects, you can build a pipeline of new clients that will continue to grow your business.

Basic Record-Keeping

Government record-keeping is a necessary part of administering your business. Fortunately, there are many choices of computer software to make the job easier. In addition to software, I strongly suggest you employ the services of a professional accountant. Pick an accountant who works with small businesses like yours. At a minimum, your accountant can file year-end forms and answer your questions. If you want to delegate more bookkeeping functions, he or she can also deposit your revenues and handle your payroll.

This chapter provides an overview of the currently required paperwork for running a small business and issuing payroll. It is not intended to substitute for the advice of an accountant.

IRS record-keeping for revenue and expenses

You must maintain records and file tax returns and other government forms to account for the revenue and expenses generated

151

in your business. Figure 15-1 provides a flowchart that shows the basic flow of information required for each type of business (sole proprietor, C corporation, or S corporation). Here's how to understand record-keeping using Figure 15-1 (Record-Keeping Flowchart):

1 The first step to generating revenue for your business occurs when you invoice your clients. Keep copies of all invoices so you can track your company's income.

2 Your client's accounts payable department processes your invoice and issues your company a payment according to the terms of your contract. If you are a sole proprietor, the client issues you IRS Form 1099 at the end of the year. You have to report all 1099 revenue on your individual tax return using IRS Form 1040.

3 When you receive a payment from a client, you deposit it in the appropriate bank account. If you are incorporated, you must deposit all revenues into a separate checking account set up for your company. If you are a sole proprietor, you can deposit revenues in your personal checking account.

4 If you are incorporated, one way you can withdraw money from the business for personal use is to issue yourself a paycheck. You can deduct the gross amount of your payroll as well as all the related payroll taxes as a corporate business expense. When you start payroll in your corporation, even if you're the only employee, you trigger a set of required state and federal payroll taxes. On the federal side, you have to file IRS Form 941 every quarter and Forms 940, W-2, and W-3 at the end of the year.

If you are a sole proprietor, as owner of the business you cannot hire yourself as an employee. When you need money from the business, you take a "draw." You don't withhold payroll taxes and you cannot deduct your draw as a business expense. On your personal taxes, you have to pay quarterly estimated federal taxes using Form 1040-ES. You also do not escape Social Security and Medicare taxes because you have to file Form 1040 Schedule SE at the end of the year to pay the self-employment tax. The IRS bases the tax on the profit your business earned (revenues minus expenses), *not* on what you withdrew from the business as an owner's

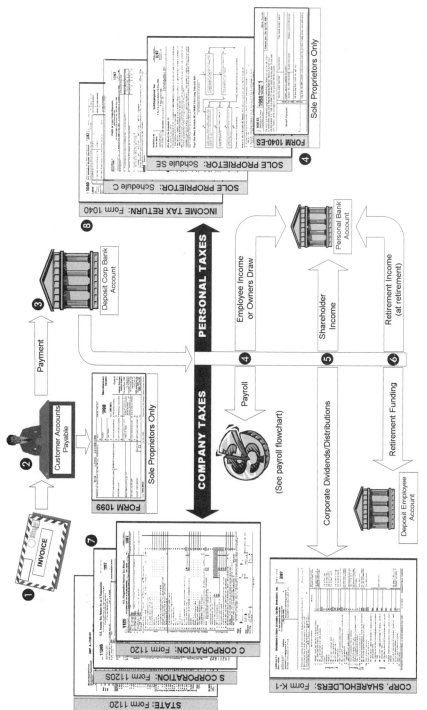

Figure 15-1: Record-keeping flowchart

draw. Social Security tax is currently 12.4 percent on the first $68,400 and Medicare is 2.9 percent on all self-employed income with no upper limit.

❺ If you are incorporated, another way to withdraw money from the business is to issue yourself a shareholder dividend. If you are an S corporation, any profit from your corporation automatically falls through to you as a shareholder in the form of a dividend. You do not pay any payroll taxes on dividends. However, you have to declare dividends as personal income and issue IRS Form K-1 to each corporate shareholder at the end of the year as part of the corporate tax return.

❻ If you are incorporated and have a company retirement plan, you must deposit the appropriate percentage of an employee's salary in their individual investment account. Some retirement plans allow the employee to participate via payroll withholding, but your company must pay any company portion of retirement funding from company funds as a business expense. As a participant in the plan, you can withdraw funds from your retirement account when you retire, according to government rules.

❼ If you are incorporated, you must file a corporate tax return at the end of the year. File IRS Form 1120S for an S corporation and IRS Form 1120 for a C corporation.

❽ If you are a sole proprietor, file a Profit or Loss from Business on IRS Form 1040 Schedule C at the end of the year with your individual income tax Form 1040.

What makes an expense?

The IRS holds that you can deduct business expenses if they meet all the following criteria:

1. You can prove the expense serves a business purpose.

2. You can provide a *notice of liability*. Examples of a notice of liability include invoices, coupon payment slips, contracts, and cashier receipts.

You can provide a *form of payment*. Examples of a form of payment include canceled checks, credit card receipts, and cashier receipts for cash payments.

3. Use credit cards issued by a bank wherever possible because of the way the IRS classifies the timing of the proof of payment. With bank credit cards, the proof of payment occurs when you *charge* an item. With non–bank-issued credit cards like those issued by retail outlets, the proof of payment occurs when you *pay* the charge. This could become important when you charge an item near the end of the year and want to include it in your expenses for that year.

Payroll record-keeping

If you are incorporated, you can either pay yourself through dividends or a salary. Although you avoid payroll taxes by paying yourself through dividends, you cannot fund a corporate retirement plan unless you issue yourself a paycheck because these plans are tied to a percentage of your gross salary. When you start a payroll, you increase the amount of required government record-keeping. Although you can do it by hand, the best way to handle the required calculations for your payroll is to get any one of several accounting software programs.

Here's how to understand payroll record-keeping using Figure 15-2 (Payroll Flowchart):

1 When you create a payroll, even if it's only to pay yourself, you must withhold certain taxes from the payee's paycheck. In addition to this, your company must pay employer payroll taxes and possibly other costs such as unemployment insurance, workers compensation, and/or state disability insurance.

2 Employee withholding includes FICA (Social Security), Medicare, federal, and state taxes. As of this writing, the rate for FICA is 6.2 percent on the first $68,400 of wages. Medicare is 1.45 percent on all wages (no upper limit). You calculate federal taxes based on the tables published in IRS Circular E. State and local taxes depend on the tax situation in your area—some states don't even have state taxes. Check with your state government to get the correct tax tables.

❸ As an employer, you must match the employee withholding amounts for FICA and Medicare. For FICA, this is 6.2 percent on the first $68,400 of wages and 1.45 percent of all wages for Medicare.

❹ Most states require employers to contribute to the state's unemployment insurance fund. This is usually a percentage of gross payroll up to a certain amount. You will likely start out with a standard rate assigned to new companies. Then, if none of your employees files unemployment claims over a period of several years, the rate declines to a minimum. For example, in Illinois, my company was charged 3.9 percent on the first $9,000 of wages for each employee. Since no employees from my company filed for unemployment insurance, my rate continued to decline each year to a rate of 0.6 percent on the first $9,000 of wages for each employee. Usually, the state requires you to file a State Employers Contribution and Wage Report each quarter along with your payment.

In addition to any state unemployment requirements, the federal government currently taxes your company 0.8 percent on the first $7,000 of wages for each employee. Assuming you earn at least $7,000, the federal tax costs you $56 a year. Once a year, you file IRS Form 940, Federal Unemployment Tax Return (FUTA), with your payment.

❺ If your company maintains a retirement program for its employees, you have to set aside employee withholding and/or company contributions for deposit in each employee's retirement account.

❻ Some states require companies to have Workers Compensation and/or State Disability Insurance for each employee. Check the requirements for your state.

❼ When you withhold federal taxes from an employee paycheck, you must regularly deposit those taxes along with the employer payroll taxes. IRS Publication Circular E describes the frequency

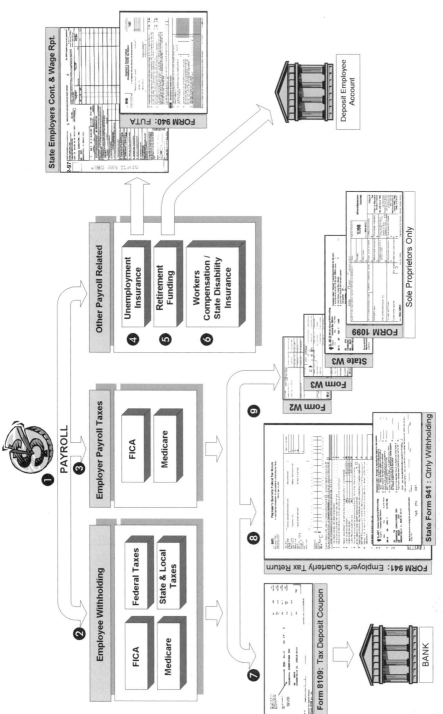

Figure 15-2: Payroll flowchart

with which you must deposit these taxes based on the size of your payroll. When you deposit these taxes, you fill out IRS Form 8109, Tax Deposit Coupon, and deposit it along with your check at any federally regulated bank.

Here's a tip. If you always deposit your taxes when you write yourself a paycheck, you're guaranteed to be current with your deposits.

8 Each quarter, you must file IRS Form 941, Employer's Quarterly Tax Return. Your state also probably has its own quarterly Form 941. On these forms you report all your payroll tax deposits for the quarter and reconcile any shortfall.

9 At the end of the year, you must issue IRS Form W-2 to each of your employees, including yourself (if you're an employee). The employee uses the W-2 to report their income on their personal tax return (Form 1040). You report the employee's income to the government by filing IRS Form W-3 and your state's Form W-3. You must also issue Form 1099-MISC to any noncorporation subcontractors if you've paid them more than $600 during the tax year.

Proposals and Contracts

"Necessity never made a good bargain."
—Benjamin Franklin (1706–1790), U.S. statesman, writer
Poor Richard's Almanack, entry for April 1735

After you've met with a client, made your pitch, and perceived interest in your service, the client will probably request that you submit a proposal. Proposals can range from a one-page summary to a multipage document. Regardless of its size, you will lean heavily on your writing and communication skills to create a proposal that walks a fine line between wetting the client's appetite and giving away the store.

If all goes well and the client accepts your proposal, you enter the contract phase of the project. In some cases, you provide the contract and in others the client will insist on using their contract. If you provide the contract, you should carefully consider if you want to write your own. Although this book does not include a specific example of a contract, there are several sources for custom-written and form contracts, including attorneys, books, software, and professional organizations. If the client or an agency provides the contract, this chapter attempts to alert you to some potentially tricky clauses. As with your bookkeeping needs, employing the services of a professional attorney familiar with business contracts may prove to be a good investment.

Proposals

In his book *The Contract and Fee-Setting Guide for Consultants & Professionals*, Howard Shenson cites survey research indicating that 95 percent of consulting projects with a value of $5,000 or more require some kind of proposal. A proposal shows clients you understand their business problem and have the expertise to solve it. For you, it acts primarily as a sales tool, but it also serves other purposes. As veteran consultant Becky Hall puts it, "For me a proposal is also the road map of the project, which I refer to when the project deviates from its original course."

In my experience, even small projects often involve a written proposal of some sort, usually a one-page letter describing the services you will deliver and what you will charge. Proposals for large, complicated projects can be labor intensive with no guarantee of success. The ability to select projects worthy of this investment and to write competent proposals are skills you must develop as a successful consultant.

The key to writing good proposals

The key to proposal writing is to remember the following.

Proposals are marketing tools. Your proposal is not a technical document where you try to impress your client with all the buzz words you know about the industry. The purpose of the proposal is to demonstrate you understand the client's situation and you can address their business problems and requirements.

Don't give away too much. Just because a client asks for a proposal, it doesn't mean they have to hire you or any consultant. If you give away too many details about how you will solve the client's problems, they may not need to hire you!

Basic proposal components

There are many ways to write proposals and there are many books on the subject. Opinions on writing a winning proposal vary as much as opinions on writing a winning resume. I've observed several basic components to a proposal. In a more formal proposal, you may create headings and a table of contents that include these components, whereas in a simple letter, you will cover these points in the letter's paragraphs. The basic components include the following.

Summary. This section is sometimes titled the Executive Summary. Its purpose is to summarize the client's current situation, requirements, and most important objectives. Try to limit the size of this section to two or three paragraphs.

Background/current situation. This section reviews the client's current situation and the factors that drove them to seek the services of an external consultant. It establishes that you understand the client's industry and problems.

Objectives/goals/scope. In this section, you itemize the specific outcome the client seeks when the project is completed. Here you establish you understand the situation. You can also use this section to specify the scope of the project (what you will and will not do).

Proposed solution/approach. Here you describe how you will bring the client from where they are now to where they want to be. Include any information that demonstrates your unique approach to the problem or any value-added methods that differentiate your services from what other consultants offer. For instance, at the end of a documentation project I offer my clients a CD-ROM recorded with all the source files.

When you write this section, you must take care not to provide an exact blueprint of how you will complete the project. Otherwise, you might just provide the client a free design document and enable them to complete the project themselves.

Deliverables. This section lists the tangible items you provide the client by the end of the project. It includes items such as reports, survey forms, training materials, documentation, electronic files, program code, and so forth.

Success enhancers. This is the section where you separate yourself from the average competitor. Here you discuss the resources you provide that add value to your services and allow you to successfully complete the project while enhancing the result. Items to include here are proprietary tools and additional services that go beyond what the client normally expects. For instance, if you developed a computer program that lets you complete portions of the project quicker than the standard manual method, you would include that information in this section.

Pricing/cost. In this section you describe the terms (fixed-fee or hourly rate) and the total estimated cost to complete the project. It is traditional to put this section at the end in a (somewhat vain) attempt to get the client to focus on the value of your solution before they consider the cost. This is a limited strategy because I have never known a recipient of a proposal who did not immediately flip to the pricing section of a proposal *first* and then return to the beginning to see the details. However, it's still probably a good idea to put the pricing in the back of the proposal.

It's also a good idea to put a time limit on the proposal. As a one-person business, you cannot afford to wait around for weeks on end without any revenue while your prospect considers your proposal. Make it clear in the proposal that you can only guarantee your schedule for a limited amount of time, after which you may not be available. This will give your prospect an additional incentive to make a prompt decision on your proposal.

Supporting materials. Optionally, you may include appendixes with supporting materials such as your brochure, technical references, and/or tables of information.

Companies and government agencies sometimes issue a formal request for proposal (RFP). They do this in an attempt to get proposals that follow a consistent format and answer their questions in a specific way so they can compare the proposals more objectively. Fully addressing the issue of RFPs is beyond the scope of this book.

Based on my experience working with two sales organizations, I've observed that by the time a client issues an RFP for a large project, they tailored it toward a specific vendor. Usually, it's a vendor with whom they have a long-standing relationship and who probably helped them write the RFP in the first place. Of course, this "stacks the deck" against any other vendors who may expend large amounts of time and effort answering the RFP. The best situation where RFPs are concerned, is to become the vendor the client consults when writing the RFP.

Proposal for Micro Widgets, Inc. Online help system for the X9 Control System

Executive Summary

Micro Widgets, Inc. desires to create an online help system for its X9 Control System that minimizes or eliminates the need for paper documentation. Micro Widgets, Inc. wants to accomplish this using RoboHelp to design a help system that minimizes calls to technical support. Logical Directions proposes to accomplish this with a three phased project that includes design, implementation, and testing. Logical Directions further proposes that Micro Widgets, Inc. consider including the services of a usability testing laboratory to ensure that the help system lives up to its full potential.

Micro Widgets, Inc.'s Objectives

Micro Widgets, Inc.'s project objectives include the following

1. Design an online help system for end users of Micro Widgets, Inc.'s X9 Control System that minimizes or eliminates the need for paper documentation.

2. Minimize calls to technical support.

3. Write online help topics for a non-technical audience of users.

4. Provide users a means of printing groups of related topics.

5. Create the online help system using RoboHelp.

6. Complete example help topics in time for Micro Widgets, Inc.'s trade show.

Approach

Logical Directions proposes a three phase approach to developing an online help system for the X9 Control System. Although this plan does not allow us to produce a completely finished help system in time for Micro Widgets, Inc.'s trade show in August, it does provide for completion of some example topics that Micro Widgets, Inc. can include for demo purposes.

12/01/98   ■ 1

Figure 16-1: Sample proposal

Phase I: Design

Logical Directions will review the X9 Control System and custom design an online help system. We propose a design team consisting of two experienced designers. During this phase the design team will accomplish the following:

1. Review the entire X9 Control System to learn its functions and intended user audience.

2. Create a layered topic design.

3. Create a list of all the help topics for the system. Note: This list is subject to revision based on changes Micro Widgets, Inc. makes to the X9 Control System software.

4. Create prototype topics for each topic category. Micro Widgets, Inc. could use these working topics for their trade show.

Phase II: Implementation

During the implementation phase, Logical Directions proposes using one person to write the topics and implement review changes. We propose two review cycles in which our consultant will do the following:

1. Write topics using RoboHelp and proprietary Logical Directions macros.

2. Submit printed topics for review using Logical Directions consolidated review forms.

3. Attend meetings with Micro Widgets, Inc. to review drafts of the help topics.

4. Implement review changes.

Phase III: Testing

Logical Directions proposes that Micro Widgets, Inc. thoroughly test the content, hypertext links, and navigational design of the help and submit corrections to us for implementation. To accomplish this, we propose a professionally designed usability study of the software and online help for the X9 Control System.

Improved usability is a key aspect to the success of a software product such as the X9 Control System. A properly implemented usability study reinforces Micro Widgets, Inc.'s goal to minimize technical support calls. The investment Micro Widgets, Inc. makes in enhancing usability will pay dividends with better performance, better industry reviews, reduced calls to technical support, and stimulated sales.

Toward this end, Logical Directions proposes that Micro Widgets, Inc. employ the services of MicroTech Usability Management. The MicroTech facility includes a fully staffed and equipped usability laboratory that includes a user room, observation room, executive viewing room, and state-of-the-art audio and video equipment.

Figure 16-1 (continued)

Deliverables

Logical Directions will provide the following deliverables to complete the project:

Design phase

Logical Directions will provide the following deliverables at the conclusion of the Design phase:

1. List of topic titles.
2. One or more working prototype topics for each major category of topic (fields, how to, etc.)

Implementation phase

Logical Directions will provide the following deliverables at the conclusion of the Implementation phase:

1. Two printed drafts for review.
2. Source and compiled help files.

Testing phase

Logical Directions will provide Source and compiled help files after implementing corrections identified during testing

Project conclusion

Logical Directions will provide a recordable CD containing final source and compiled help files

Success Enhancers

Logical Directions will employ various value-added resources to successfully complete the project. In addition to these resources Logical Directions proposes options for Micro Widgets, Inc.'s consideration.

Logical Directions will employ the following tools, procedures, and techniques to advance successful project completion.

Macros to assist the layered approach
Logical Directions has developed proprietary Microsoft Word VBA macros that automate creation of layered topics connected to each major topic. This benefits Micro Widgets, Inc. by accelerating the labor-intensive task of creating topics.

Project files delivered on recordable CD
At the conclusion of the project, Logical Directions provides a recordable CD with all project source files and related data. This benefits Micro Widgets, Inc. with documentation version control and a fixed-form backup of the project source files at the point the project was completed.

Figure 16-1 (continued)

Proposal for Micro Widgets, Inc.   **12/01/98**

Pricing Proposal

We propose completing this project on a time-and-materials basis. This gives Micro Widgets, Inc. the flexibility to make changes in the X9 Control System and adjust associated project hours. Since the exact hours expended will vary, we base our proposal on a range of hours. Our proposal includes two experienced technical communicators and the value added resources discussed in the section on Success Enhancers. Based on this, we estimate a total cost of $39,900.00 depending on contingencies and options.

Pricing

The table below summarizes the pricing schedule for all phases of the project:

Phase	Rate/hr	Hours	Amount
Phase I: Design			
Consultant 1	70	40	$2,800.00
Consultant 2	65	40	$2,600.00
Phase II: Implementation			
Consultant 1	70	300	$21,000.00
10% Contingency	70	30	$2,100.00
Phase III: Testing			
Consultant 1	70	20	$1,400.00
Usability testing	†	†	$10,000.00†
Total:	—	430	$39,900.00

†Estimated. Exact hours and pricing to be provided by MicroTech Usability Management.

Assumptions

The Pricing Proposal is based on the following assumptions:

1. The X9 Control System consists of approximately 75 screens. The estimated time to complete two drafts of each topic during the Implementation phase is 4 hours producing a total of approximately 300 hours to complete the Implementation phase.

2. The Pricing Proposal includes a 10% contingency buffer for the Implementation phase.

3. MicroTech Services Usability Management will provide hourly estimates and pricing for the Usability Testing option.

Logical Directions, Inc.   ■ 4

Figure 16-1 (continued)

Contracts

After the client accepts your proposal there's still one more thing you have to do between popping the champagne in celebration and starting work on the client's project. You and the client must enter into a contractual agreement. Regardless of whether you formally call it a contract or a letter of agreement, it's important that you *always* create a written set of terms that both you and the client agree upon before beginning the work.

The goals of a contract

You should approach contracts with the following goals in mind.

Avoid misunderstandings. A written contract helps you and the client avoid misunderstandings by making sure you both agree on the project's basic assumptions. This means you must carefully outline exactly what you will and will not deliver as part of the agreement. When you describe the scope of the project, you want to anticipate and address any potential conflict-producing situations.

Define your status. The contract should clearly define your relationship with the client or agency. As an independent contractor, the contract should reinforce the fact that you are not a permanent employee of the client or agency and therefore cannot participate in any employee benefits.

Assure payment. A properly executed contract establishes your legal right to collect payment for services you've delivered. It also defines how and when the client will pay you.

Minimize liability. As mentioned earlier, errors and omissions insurance in a nonregulated field is often unavailable or priced beyond the means of many consultants. Because of this, the contract is your first defense against honest mistakes you might make delivering your services to the client. The contract should clearly define your responsibilities and those of the client. It should also define any dependent circumstances beyond your control which could impact the success of the project. Some contracts include a Limited Warranty section for this purpose.

Avoid litigation. One of the best uses of a contract is to head off disputes that can grow into expensive litigation. There are two common disputes that arise between contractor and client. The first occurs when the client believes the contractor didn't deliver a quality job. The second is when the client doesn't pay the contractor for work that isn't in dispute. One popular way to mitigate contract disputes out of court is to include a clause calling for binding arbitration according to the rules of the American Arbitration Association. This allows an arbitrator rather than a court to settle disputes between consultant and client.

Basic contract components

Contracts can vary considerably, but there are some basic components that recur in independent consultant contracts. Some clauses only apply to contracts with agencies.

Relationship of parties. Sometimes a contract covers this in a Consultant and Independent Contractor section. This establishes you are an independent contractor, not an employee.

Scope of work. This is where you define what services and/or products you will and will not deliver to the client. Sometimes, you can refer to the information in a detailed proposal to describe the scope of the project. You might also define what the procedure is for changing the scope or adding new work not originally defined. This section may also describe the process by which the client approves completed work.

Compensation. The compensation section of a contract establishes how much and when the client pays you. You may also use this section to itemize those incidental expenses you will pass through to the client such as delivery services, postage, copy charges, long distance telephone charges, and travel expenses.

If you bill on an hourly basis, you usually state the hourly rate and the frequency at which you will invoice the client. The frequency can be a regular period of time such as weekly, biweekly, or monthly, or according to specific milestones in the project.

If you based the project on a fixed-fee, you should break up the payments. It's typical to break fixed-fee projects into thirds where you receive one-third when the contract is signed, one-third at some milestone in the middle of the project, and one-third when you deliver your final finished product.

Proprietary rights. This part of a contract defines who owns the tangible results of your work, including copyrights and patents. Most consultant contracts are Work for Hire agreements, where the client receives the right to the finished work provided the client has properly paid the consultant according to the contract terms. You may, however, want to retain rights to "background technology" you commonly use over and over with all your clients provided you own the rights to the technology or you license the rights with a right to sublicense. For example, if you are a programmer, you may have a library of common program subroutines you developed to make your work more efficient. Or you may be a psychologist who developed or licensed a standard psychological test you use as part of your consulting service. In these cases, you must be careful not to give away the rights to use these technologies with future clients.

Cancellation. The cancellation or termination clause in a contract defines under what circumstances either party can end the contract before the project is completed. Usually, this clause identifies general circumstances in which one party has strayed from the terms of the contract and a period of time during which the problem can be corrected (usually 30 days). If the problem is not corrected, the offended party can terminate the contract, usually by sending written notice to the other party.

Noncompete clause. You will usually only see this type of clause in an agency contract. The purpose of this clause is to protect the agency's investment in marketing and client relations after you complete work for one of their clients. It restricts you, for a period of time, from contracting directly with the agency's client for whom you are doing work on behalf of the agency. A typical noncompete period of time is one year. The time period usually begins when you complete the client project. If the client is a large corporation with many departments, you should try to restrict the scope of the noncompete just to that department, so you are free to contract with other departments or divisions of the client company.

In some cases, a client other than an agency may include a noncompete clause that restricts you from working with competitors for a period of time. The period may just be during the project or may continue for a period after you complete the project.

Hold harmless clause. Some clients require this section, which holds them harmless against your losses and liabilities resulting from injuries, death, damage to property, or theft while you work on the project. Clients may require that you agree to maintain liability, workers compensation, or other insurance while working on the project.

Disputes/remedies. This section of the contract explains how you and the client will handle contract disputes. A popular method to handle disputes and avoid court litigation is to include a clause in the contract that commits both parties to mediation or binding arbitration under the rules of the American Arbitration Association.

Liability. The liability section of the contract restricts your liability for the client's lost profits or incidental or consequential damages from your work on the project. This section may include discussion of your "warranties," "representations," or "guarantees." Basic guarantees you can offer include assurance that you have the authority to enter into a contract with the client and that you will not infringe on any copyright, patent, or trade secret.

When should you consult an attorney to review a contract?

If you have a well-tested form contract that you supply to the client and the client does not demand any drastic changes, you can probably create the document without consulting an attorney. If the client prefers that you use their contract or if they want to make significant changes to your contract, you might want to consult your attorney. A good rule of thumb is that if the value of the contract is $10,000 or more, it's probably worth having an attorney review the document before you sign.

Sources for contracts

Following are some sources for contracts.

Attorneys. To make sure you create a form contract that's really customized to your situation, you should use an attorney.

Although you'll pay an initial fee to create a form contract, you can use it over and over again.

Books. Several books on contracts and consulting include boilerplate contracts. A good source of self-help law books including contracts is Nolo Press (800-992-6656).

Software. Several companies market software that asks you several questions and then generates a contract by filling in the blanks. You must be careful not to make significant changes to these contracts once they are generated by the software so as not to invalidate any important clauses.

Organizations. Many professional organizations provide attorney-approved contracts to their members. For instance, both the Independent Computer Consultants Association (ICCA) and the National Writers Union offer contracts to their members.

Delivering Your Service

"Or those who have improved life by the knowledge they have found out, and those who have made themselves remembered by some for their services: round the brows of all these is worn a snow-white band."

—Virgil (70–19 B.C.), Roman poet.

What are the real assets of your business? It's not your equipment and office furniture and it's not the money you have in your business bank account. One set of your business assets includes your reputation and the "good will" you build with your clients. The other key set of assets for your business is your prospect and client list.

Building and maintaining prospect and client information

Prospects are people or companies who may be interested in your services, but who have not contracted with you yet. Clients are people or companies with whom you've contracted at least once.

It will take you some time to build your prospect and client list. Its value lies in its ability to provide additional work through new projects and referrals to new customers. If you publish a newsletter as part of your business, it provides you with a sub-

173

scription list. If you are fortunate enough to build your business into a multimillion dollar consulting firm with a staff of professionals, other larger consulting firms may offer to buy your firm. They'll do this to obtain two things, your staff of qualified consultants and your client list.

Consequently, you should collect and maintain a minimum amount of information about your clients. There are many contact management software packages that can help you in this effort. A simple paper form like the one shown in the figure is good enough to start. As a matter of fact, it's not a bad idea to maintain a paper contact form even if you use contact manager software. It keeps you prepared for when you contact a client without your computer and you can always enter the information into your contact manager later on.

Start collecting client information immediately when a prospect calls you to inquire about your services. The following is a minimal list of the type of information you should collect from your clients.

Reference information. Create a keyword or keywords you can use to reference this prospect in the future. It may be the name of the prospect contact or the name of the company. Enter the date they first called you. Most important, ask them how they were referred to you. This gives you valuable feedback on your marketing efforts. Did they find you through an advertisement or were they referred to you by someone?

Client business information. Enter the prospect or client's formal business name and the type of business and industry.

Client office information. Enter standard communication information including the prospect's address, fax number, and Web page address. Since you will probably schedule a face-to-face meeting with the prospect, write directions to the prospect's office.

Client contact information. Enter the name, phone number, address (if different from the office address), fax number, and email address of the person who will act as your contact in the prospect company.

Contact Information

Ref:_____   Date of first contact:_____

How Referred: _____

Client Information

Business Name:_____

Contact Name: _____   Phone: _____

Address: _____   Fax: _____

_____   EMail: _____

Web Address: _____

Agency Information

Business Name:_____

Contact Name: _____   Phone: _____

Address: _____   Fax: _____

_____   EMail: _____

Web Address: _____

Project Profile

Project Description: _____

_____

_____

_____

_____

Tools Needed:_____

_____

_____

Work Location: ❑ Onsite: _____%   ❑ Home: _____%

Est. Delivery Date: _____   Rate Quoted: $_____   Project Value:$_____

Figure 17-1: Sample contact form

Agency information. If you connected to the client or prospect through an agency, enter the agency's contact name, address, phone number, fax number, email, and Web page address. Make note of the agency's standard noncompete period. Ask the agency if the noncompete applies to the entire client company or just to the department where you will be working.

Project information. Write a description of the prospect's project. You will have to customize additional project information depending on your services and the industry in which you operate. I suggest using checklists to help define the scope of the project. For example, as a technical communicator, I use a checklist that includes the type of technical document the prospect needs (user guide, administrator guide, online help, and so forth), the audience for the publication (end users, programmers, administrators, management, and so forth), and the type of production software the prospect prefers.

Although you will customize project checklists for your own situation, there is some information that is common to most projects, including the required deadline, the work location (at the client's site or at your office), and whether they have used consultants for this type of work before. If you quoted them a rate, you should make a note of that also.

Working with clients

Once you start getting projects, you need some basic rules-of-thumb so you can productively work with clients.

Don't misrepresent yourself. When talking to potential clients, there are several ways you can misrepresent yourself. You could elevate some light skills to expert status. You could overbook yourself giving each client the impression that you are available to spend more time than you really can on their project. In a competitive bidding situation, you could propose that the project will take fewer hours than you know it will really take. Avoid all of these unethical traps. You wipe out any short-term gain when the client realizes you misrepresented yourself. Then your reputation is tarnished. As consultants, our reputation is all we have. Once that's gone, you're history!

Prepare the client. If you anticipate spending a significant amount of time at the client's location during completion of a project, you should prepare the client for your stay. This is as much to their advantage as yours. For instance, I once showed up to start writing documentation for a project and the client had not informed the security guard I was expected. I had to wait nearly an hour while security located my client contact so they could admit me. Since the project was on an hourly basis, the client was charged for my time while I waited. If the project you're working on is a fixed-bid, it's even more important the client is ready to work with you because any nonproductive time spent on the project increases the cost of the project to you.

You can try to avoid some of these problems by providing the client with the following preparation checklist before starting the project.

❑ Set up security access to the building.

❑ Set up company communications such as telephone, email, and voice mail.

❑ Set up security access to the computer network.

❑ Provide appropriate equipment and software and company reference materials relevant to the project (style guides, company reports, organizational charts, and so forth).

❑ Prepare express mail envelopes with client's account filled in for offsite transit of materials to the client.

❑ Provide email or Internet address for transit of electronic files to the client.

Behave like a guest, not an employee. When you work at the client's site, you must exercise restraint. Avoid complaining about your accommodations, company policy, or company employees. Wise consultants avoid putting themselves in the middle of the client's internal politics.

Maintain contact with the client. Make sure the client is always aware of the status of the project. You can do this through periodic written status reports and/or meetings with your client contact. Make it your business to make sure the client is not blindsided by a major problem with the project. Afterward, follow up with the client periodically.

Avoid conflicts of interest. Don't accept commissions or finder's fees from vendors you recommend without disclosing this relationship to your client. If you hold office or occupy a controlling interest in a company competing with the client or a vendor company, you should inform the client. Avoid openly recruiting the client's employees to work for you outside the client's company, especially during a client project. Finally, maintain a professional business relationship with client employees and other contractors while you are working on a client project. For instance, it's best to avoid dating a client employee or contractor during the project period.

After you complete the project

A week or two after you complete a project, it's a good idea to follow up with the client to make sure they are satisfied with your work. This is a good time to debrief the client on what they liked and what they wished you had done better. If the client is satisfied, request to use them as a reference. If they are not completely satisfied, try to find out exactly why and then try to correct the problem by offering some free consulting hours or a discount on their final bill. To assist in gathering information about client satisfaction, I've developed a post-project survey form I submit to clients shortly after project completion.

TWrite, Inc.
Post-project Satisfaction Survey

Company: .... **Date:** ....

1. Are you satisfied with the services provided by TWrite for your project:

   ❑ Yes   ❑ No

2. If no, please explain below:

   _____

   _____

   _____

   _____

3. What did you like best about the services provided by TWrite?

   _____

   _____

   _____

   _____

4. If you have any suggestions for improvement, please specify below:

   _____

   _____

   _____

   _____

5. Can TWrite use you as a reference?

   ❑ Yes   ❑ No

6. Can you provide a quote that we can use in our marketing materials?

   _____

   _____

   _____

   _____

   _____

7. Would you recommend TWrite to a colleague?

   ❑ Yes   ❑ No

8. Are there any colleagues, friends, or other contacts you can refer to TWrite? If so, please list them below:

Name	Phone Number/Email

Thank you for completing our survey. We look forward to working with you again!

Rev. 11/18/98

Figure 17-2: Sample post-project survey form

Final Thoughts

"Either you think—or else others have to think for you and take power from you, pervert and discipline your natural tastes, civilize and sterilize you."

—F. Scott Fitzgerald (1896–1940), U.S. author
Nicole's thoughts, in *Tender is the Night* (1934)

After you've been doing independent consulting for a while, it gets into your blood. It seems there is some imaginary line you cross after which you never want to return to conventional employment, despite the hassles associated with running your own business. I know more than one independent consultant who closed their business and became an employee for someone else, only to quit and return to independent consulting in a couple years. If you stick with this business long enough, you'll likely reach that point as well. Here are some tips for success on the road toward that point of no return.

Be committed

To succeed in this business, you must be totally committed. If you view independent consulting as simply "something to do between jobs" your heart will not be in it and the people you deal with will sense this. Independent consulting is challenging and it's easy to get discouraged. When you don't have a project, time seems to stand still. Use this time to double your marketing efforts and invest in additional training for yourself.

Differentiate yourself

Make sure you stand apart from others who offer similar services and identify how you add value to your services. Articulate any unique methodology or skill that separates you from the average consultant in your field. Focus on value rather than price. You will quickly put yourself out of business if you compete for projects based solely on price.

Find the client's needs

Every project is a custom job. Listen hard for what the client really *needs*. Sometimes even the client has difficulty articulating this, so you'll have to listen carefully and ask intelligent questions.

Invest in your image

Although you are a small business, you must project confidence through your business image. You do this through your dress, logo, resume, proposals, and presentations. You can project a professional business image without being extravagant. If necessary, get help designing your logo and promotional materials from a graphic artist and/or writer. Attend classes in proposal writing and giving presentations. Think of these items as the "lighted sign" in front of your business. You don't want anyone to see the sign when it's dirty and has several light bulbs burned out.

Invest in your skills

Some career counselors suggest you should invest at least 7 percent of your income every year to learn more about your industry. Spend time to stay current and learn new skills required for your business. Subscribe to trade magazines and professional journals. Attend professional conferences and seminars. Schedule yourself for refresher classes.

Find a mentor

If possible, try to find someone with greater experience than you who can take you under his or her wing and serve as an advisor and friend. This is particularly helpful when you are getting started, but you can benefit from a mentor all through your business career. Some professional organizations and universities provide organized mentor programs that match people in your industry with a more experienced practitioner.

Network, network, network

The more people you meet the better. Network at professional meetings, career fairs, and social events. Without becoming obnoxious, you should consider even friends and colleagues as potential sources of business. These contacts may hire you themselves or provide useful referrals.

Solicit endorsements

Extend your reach by asking clients and other contacts to act as references or to provide endorsements and testimonials. These supporting statements help prospects feel safe doing business with you. After you complete a project and are sure the client is satisfied, follow up with a request to write about the experience.

Keep in touch

There's a rule in sales called the 80/20 rule. This rule assumes that 80 percent of your business comes from 20 percent of your clients. When you consider the cost in time and expense of marketing to prospects who don't know you, you appreciate the value of getting a new project from an existing client. Keep in touch with your client base. Don't wait for them to call you. Call your current clients periodically to see how they are doing. Many clients are so swamped they don't have time to call for help, so your call can open the door to some new business. Some consultants offer free follow-up checks sometime after completing a project to assess the results of the project. Don't let your clients think you have forgotten about them as soon as their project ends.

Give 110 percent

Finally, always deliver a little more than what your client expects. Identify any valuable extras you can deliver that require a little extra effort on your part but reinforce your relationship with the client.

Bibliography

Baldwin, Ben G. *The Complete Book of Insurance*. Chicago: Probes Publishing Company, 1991.

Csikszentmihalyi, Mihaly. *Flow: The Psychology of Optimal Experience*. New York: Harper and Row, 1990.

Darby III, Joseph B. "The Untouchable Topic: Agency Fees," *Contract Professional*. July/August 1998.

Holtz, Herman. *How to Succeed as an Independent Consultant*. New York: John Wiley & Sons, 1988.

Kintler, David. *Independent Consulting*. Holbrook, MA: Adams Media Corporation, 1998.

Krunemaker, Larry. "Searching for Affordable Health Insurance." *Home-Office Computing*. March 1993.

National Business Employment Weekly. *Networking*. New York: John Wiley & Sons, 1994

Ruhl, Janet. *The Computer Consultant's Guide*. New York: John Wiley & Sons, 1994.

———. "Workbook: How to Determine Your Going Rate." *Contract Professional*. March/April 1997.

Shenson, Howard L. *The Contract and Fee-Setting Guide for Consultants & Professionals*. New York: John Wiley & Sons, 1990.

Stoll, Cliff. *The Cuckoo's Egg*. New York: Pocket Books, 1990.

Zanger, Larry M. "The Possible Reclassification of Computer Consultants, Part I." *Chicago Computer Guide*. October 1989.

——. "Computer Consultants Status May Change, Part II." *Chicago Computer Guide*. November 1989.

Recommended Resources

Consulting

Holtz, Herman. *How to Start and Run a Writing & Editing Business*. New York: John Wiley & Sons, 1992. ISBN 0-471-54831-6. In this book Mr. Holtz focuses on consulting as a writer/editor.

——. *How to Succeed as an Independent Consultant*. New York: John Wiley & Sons, 1988. ISBN 0-471-84729-1. Mr. Holtz wrote the definitive text on consulting. Of particular interest is his information on marketing to government institutions.

Juillet, Christopher. *The Meter Is Running and Other Essays on Consulting*. Ann Arbor, MI: Communications Professionals, 1991. Mr. Juillet's 45-page booklet contains several excellent essays on independent consulting including subjects on rate setting and life as an independent. You can reach him by telephone at 734-913-2430, via fax at 734-913-2450, or on the Web at www.cjuillet.com.

Karasik, Paul. *How to Make It BIG in the Seminar Business*. New York: McGraw-Hill. ISBN 0-07-034120-6. This is an excellent, well-written book on developing and marketing seminars for your business.

Kent, Peter. *Making Money in Technical Writing*. New York: Arco Pub, 1997. ISBN 0-028-61883-1. If you're interested in starting a consulting business as a technical writer, this is a good book to read. It is an update to Mr. Kent's *Technical Writer's Freelancing Guide* published in 1992.

Kintler, David. *Adams Streetwise Independent Consulting*. Holbrook, MA: Adams Media Corporation, 1998. ISBN: 1-55850-728-0. This book is part of the Adams Streetwise® series. It contains several excellent examples of business plans and proposals.

Kraft, Herbert R. *How I Sold a Million Copies of My Software*. Holbrook, MA: Adams Media Corporation, 1997. ISBN 1-55850-724-8. If you create your own software and ever wondered how to sell it, this is the book to read.

Ruhl, Janet. *The Computer Consultants Guide*. New York: John Wiley & Sons, 1994. ISBN 0-47159-661-2. If you are considering a business as a computer consultant, you *must* get this book. A computer consultant herself, Ms. Ruhl lead CompuServe's computer consultant forum from which she draws much of the research for her book.

———. *The Computer Consultants Workbook*. Levererett, MA: Technion Books, 1996. ISBN 0-9647116-0-5. An excellent companion to Ms. Ruhl's other books. She provides worksheets to help potential computer consultants prepare their business.

Shenson, Howard L. *The Contract and Fee-Setting Guide for Consultants & Professionals*. New York: John Wiley & Sons, 1990. ISBN 0-471-51538-8. This book takes a textbook approach to contracts and setting fees. In addition to these subjects, it also discusses proposals.

Whitmyer, Claude, Salli Raspberry, and Michael Phillips. *Running a One-Person Business*. Berkeley, CA: Ten Speed Press, 1989. ISBN 0-898-15237-2. This book provides the basics for starting and operating a business when you are the only employee.

Certifications

Christianson, Scott and Ava Fajen. *Computer and Network Professional's Certification Guide*. Sybex, 1997. ISBN 0-78212-260-4. This book is directed at computer and network professionals of all levels of experience. It covers more than 70 vendor- and organization-based certification programs.

Martinez, Anne. *Get Certified and Get Ahead*. New York: McGraw-Hill, 1998. ISBN 0-07041-127-1. This book provides information about more than 170 computer certifications including A+, Adobe, C++, Certified Computing Professional (CCP), Certified Internet Webmaster, Cisco, Microsoft, Novell, PowerBuilder, Java, Lotus, SAP, Visual Basic, and more. It also provides listings of Web sites, books, magazines, and information on more than 40 vendors of preparation materials to help you get certified.

Mueller, John Paul and Anthony Gatlin (contributor). *The Complete Microsoft Certification Success Guide*. New York: McGraw-Hill, 1997. ISBN: 0-07913-201-4 Coauthored by a Microsoft insider, this complete guide to all of Microsoft's certifications includes an interactive CD with assessment tests for the most popular exams.

Geocertify, www.geocertify.com. Provides news and resources for computer professionals seeking to get certified or products from various computer vendors.

Transcender, www.transcender.com. Sells self study and simulation software to prepare for Microsoft certification exams.

Accounting, Insurance, and Legal Issues

American Arbitration Association Website. www.adr.org. Provides information on using arbitration rather than litigation to settle contractual disputes.

Baldwin, Ben G. *The Complete Book of Insurance*. Chicago: Probes Publishing Company. ISBN: 1-55738-235-2. This book tries to cut through the confusion surrounding all forms of personal insurance including medical, disability, liability, and life.

Crawford, Tad. *Business & Legal Forms for Authors & Self-Publishers*. New York: Allworth Press, 1990. ISBN 0-927629-03-8. This book is filled with useful forms for writers and self-publishers including an author-agent contract, book publishing contract, and permission form.

Fishman, Stephen. *Software Development: A Legal Guide.* Berkeley, CA: Nolo Press, 1994. ISBN 0-87337-209-3. This is an excellent book if you develop software and want to protect your intellectual property. It includes a diskette with form contracts and agreements.

Jenkins, Michael D. and the Entrepreneurial Services Group of Ernst & Young. *Starting and Operating a Business in* (your state). Grants Pass, OR: The Oasis Press®/PSI Research, 1991. ISBN varies with state version. This is a comprehensive guide to laws regarding small businesses in your state. The publishers print this guide for many states and regularly update it; check for the most recent revision.

Kamoroff, Bernard, C.P.A. *Small-Time Operator.* Laytonville, CA: Bell Springs Publishing, 1996. ISBN 0-917510-06-2. This book should be a permanent part of your business library. It's an excellent guide to bookkeeping for a small company written for the layman. Mr. Kamoroff updates this book regularly to keep up with changing tax laws.

Parsons Technology, Inc. 1700 Progress Drive, PO Box 100, Hiawatha, IA 52233-0100; 800-779-6000; www.parsonstech.com. Sells legal software for personal and business use.

Techinsurance, 333 West Campbell Road, Suite 150, Richardson, TX 75081, 972-231-1509 or 800-668-7020; Fax 972-497-9804; www.techinsurance.com. Techinsurance specializes in package liability and property insurance policies for information technology contractors (programmers, software developers, Web designers, and so forth). Their package liability coverage includes general business liability, Worker's Compensation, and professional liability (errors and omissions).

Internet

Davis, Jack and Susan Merritt (Contributor). *The Web Design Wow Book.* Peachpit Press, 1998. ISBN 0-20108-8678-2. This book includes a CD-ROM and provides an inspirational range of tips and techniques on designing an appealing Web site.

Flanders, Vincent and Michael Willis. *Web Pages that Suck*. Sybex, 1998. ISBN 0-2018-8678-2. This book takes a humorous approach to teaching good Web site design by reviewing badly designed sites and then showing how they could be improved with a site "makeover." The authors also maintain a website on the same subject at www.webpagesthatsuck.com.

Lemay, Larura. *Teach Yourself Web Publishing with HTML in a Week*. Indianapolis, IN: SAMS Publishing. ISBN 0-672-30667-0. If you are willing to try "getting your hands dirty" with HyperText Markup Language (HTML), this book can show you how to build a more customized Web site.

Shafran, Andy and Todd Stauffer. *Creating Your Own America Online Web Pages*. Indianapolis, IN: Que Corp, 1996. ISBN 0-7897-0901-5. If you're not an Internet expert and you have an account with AOL, this is an easy-to-understand guide for designing and creating your own Web site with a minimum of fuss.

Marketing

Computer Consultant's Resource Page. www.realrates.com. Web site maintained by Janet Ruhl, the author of The Computer Consultants Guide. In addition to articles about consulting in the Information Technology (IT) field, Ms. Ruhl publishes the results of consultant surveys that include IT consulting rates and agency markups.

Davidson, Jeffrey P. *Marketing for the Home-Based Business*. Holbrook, MA: Bob Adams, 1990. ISBN 1-55850-945-3. This book focuses on projecting a high-level image from your home office. It discusses using your computer, fax, and copier to market your business.

Levinson, Jay Conrad and Charles Rubin. *Guerrilla Marketing Online Weapons*. New York: Houghton Mifflin. 1996. ISBN: 0-395-77019-X. This book in the *Guerilla Marketing* series provides 100 low-cost methods for marketing a small business on the Internet and through email.

―――. *Guerrilla Marketing Weapons*. New York: Plume. 1990. ISBN 0-452-26519-3. This book in the *Guerilla Marketing* series provides 100 low-cost methods for marketing a small business.

National Business Employment Weekly. *Networking*. New York: John Wiley & Sons, Inc, 1994. ISBN 0-471-31026-3. Although the publisher directs this book primarily to job seekers, it contains useful information for networking as a small business.

Organizations

The American Association of Political Consultants
   900 Second St., Suite 204
   Washington, DC 20002
   202-37-9585
   www.theaapc.org

American Association of Professional Consultants
   (AAPC)
   3577 Fourth Avenue San Diego, CA 92103
   619-297-2210
   www.consultapc.org

American Consultants League
   1290 North Palm Avenue
   Sarasota, FL 34236
   813-952-9290
   http://expert-market.com/consultant/resource/acl.html

American Society of Agricultural Consultants
   950 S. Cherry St., Suite 508
   Denver, CO 80246-2664
   303-759-5091
   www.agri-associations.org/asac/

Association of Bridal Consultants
   200 Chestnutland Road
   New Milford, CT
   06776-2521
   860-355-0464
   www.trainingforum.com/ASN/ABC/

Association of Executive Search Consultants
   500 Fifth Avenue, Suite 930
   New York, NY 10110
   212-398-9560
   www.aesc.org/

Association of Image Consultants (AIC)
   509 Madison Avenue, Suite 1400
   New York, New York 10022
   212-642-9009
   http://www.aici.org/

Council of Consulting Organizations (CCO)
   521 5th Avenue, 35th Floor
   New York, NY 10175
   212-697-9693

Independent Computer
Consultants Association
   11131 South Towne Square
   Suite F
   St. Louis, MO 63123
   800-774-4222 / 314-892-1675
   www.icca.org/

International Public Relations
Association, (U.S. IPRA)
   McCormick & Co, Inc.
   18 Loveton Circle,
   Sparks, MD 21152
   410-771-7301
   http://www.ipranet.org/

National Association for the
Self-Employed (NASE)
   2121 Precinct Line Road
   Hurst, TX 76054
   800-232-NASE
   www.nase.org

National Bureau of
Certified Consultants
Management Consulting Center
   2728 Fifth Avenue, San
   Diego, CA 92103
   619-297-2207
   www.national-bureau.com

National Speakers Association
   1500 S. Priest Dr.
   Tempe, AZ 85281
   602-976-2552
   www.nsaspeaker.org

National Writer's Union
   National Office East
   113 University Place
   6th Floor
   New York, NY 10003
   212-254-0279
   Fax 212-254-0673
   Email nwu@nwu.org
   www.nwu.oreg

National Writers Union
   National Office West
   337 17th Street, #101
   Oakland, CA 94612
   510-839-0110
   Fax 510-839-6097
   Email nwu@nwu.org

Project Management Institute
   130 South State Road
   Upper Darby, PA 19082
   610-734-3330
   www.pmi.org/

Public Relations Society
of America (PRSA)
   33 Irving Pl, 3rd Floor
   New York, NY 10003-2376
   212-995-2230
   www.prsa.org/

Society for Technical
Communication (STC)
   901 North Stuart Street,
   Suite 904
   Arlington, Virginia
   22203-1854
   703-522-4114
   www.stc-va.org

Toastmasters International
P.O. Box 9052
Mission Viejo, CA 92690
714-858-8255
Email tminfo@toastmasters.org
www.toastmasters.org

Turnaround Management
Association (TMA)
14800 Conference Center
Drive, Suite 402
Chantilly, VA 22021
703-803-8301
www.turnaround.org

Periodicals

Contract Employment Weekly
CE Publications, Inc.
P.O. Box 97000
Kirkland, WA 98083
206-823-2222
www.ceweekly.wa.com

*Contract Professional
Magazine*
125 Walnut Street
Watertown, MA 02172
800-297-6932
Email conpro@shore.net
www.contractpro.com

An outstanding publication published quarterly and slanted toward the technical consultant. Contains articles specific to contracting and independent consulting on subjects such as setting rates, contracts, and agencies. Each issue contains an article spotlighting consulting in a particular region of the country.

Home Office Computing
156 West 56th St., New
York, NY 10019
800-288-7812
Email lettershoc@aol.com
www.smalloffice.com

Technical Employment News
PD News
Publications &
Communications, Inc.
P.O. Box 399
Cedar Park, TX 7813-9987
800-678-9724

Although this publication is primarily targeted toward contract engineers, subscribers receive the *Directory of Technical Service Firms* listing agencies who hire a wide range of technical professionals. *PD News* will mail a subscriber's one-page resume to about forty agencies as part of your subscription.

The WinHelp Journal
  WinWriters
  3415 Soundview Drive West
  Seattle, WA 98199
  Email journal@winwriters.com
  www.winwriters.com

  Previously published as a paper magazine, this publication is now exclusively published on the Web. Subscribers enter a username and password to gain access. Provides a resource directory of online help developers. Subscribers can list their business in the directory at no additional cost.

Government Resources

Internal Revenue Service
  www.irs.ustreas.gov
  You can download tax forms and tax preparation documents from this Web site.

Small Business Administration
  www.sbaonline.sba.gov

Business Resources

Intuit Inc.
  www.intuit.com
  Provides information about Quicken and Quickbooks as well as articles on management and accounting. Also provides links to Dow Jones News Service and the Better Business Bureau.

Small Business Law Center
  www.courttv.com/legalhelp/business
  Provides legal discussions and assistance for locating a lawyer by location and specialty. Court TV maintains the site.

Small Business Resource Center
  www.Webcom.com/seaquest/sbrc/welcome.html
  Provides a guide to small business sites on the Internet such as online newsletters, venture capital firms, publishers, and trade associations.

Womenbiz

www.womenbiz.net/

Provides information for female business owners.

HTML editing programs

HyperText Markup Language (HTML) is the code that tells your browser software where and how to display text, graphics, and other elements of a Web site. You can enter HTML commands (called "tags") yourself using any text editor. However, this is tedious so there are many HTML editor programs available through the Internet that make the job easier. Most of the companies and individuals who develop HTML editors offer free or inexpensive shareware versions and more robust "pro" versions of their software for a larger price. Most of the following HTML editor programs are available for Microsoft Windows and Macintosh systems:

BBEdit
   www.barebones.com/
   bbedit.html

FrontPage
   www.microsoft.com

Home Page
   www.claris.com

HotDog
   www.sausage.com

HoTMetal
   www.softquad.com

HTML Assistant
   www.brooknorth.com

HTML Writer
   www.public.asu.edu/
   ~bottger/

HTMLed
   www.ist.ca

PageMill
   www.adobe.com

Web Home Page Host Sites

The following sites provide free or inexpensive space to host your Web site (see Chapter 12 for more information):

GeoCities
   www.geocities.com

Angelfire Communications
   www.angelfire.com

Tripod
   www.tripod.com

XOOM
   www.xoom.com

The following site provides Internet registration services to register your own unique domain name and forward visitors to the actual location of your Web site (see Chapter 12 for more information):

NameSecure
www.namesecure.com

Web Search Engines

The following Web sites provide search engines and/or registration services for your Web page. See Chapter 12 for more information on using Web search engines.

AltaVista
www.altavista.com

Excite
www.excite.com

HotBot
www.hotbot.com

InfoSeek
infoseek.com

Lycos
www.lycos.com/

OpenText
www.opentext.com/

Submit It!
www.submit-it.com/

This is a free service that makes it easier to submit your URL to multiple search engines. It allows you to register with more than 15 different services by filling out one form.

WebCrawler
www.webcrawler.com/

Yahoo!
www.yahoo.com/

Internet Job Boards

The following Web sites allow you to search for employment openings throughout the country. Some specialize in contract employment while others specialize in permanent positions.

The Computer Jobs Store
www.computerjobs.com

ConsultLink
www.consultlink.com

Data Processing Independent Consultants Exchange (DICE)
www.dice.com

Job Options
www.joboptions.com

JobBank USA
www.jobbankusa.com

MacTalent
www.mactalent.com
This site specializes in
Apple Macintosh profes-
sionals.

MedSearch
www.medsearch.com
This site specializes in
health care professionals.

The Monster Board
www.monster.com

Tri-State Jobs
www.tristatejobs.com

This site covers jobs and contracts in Connecticut, New
York, and New Jersey.

Job fairs

The following commercial career fair companies organize job
fairs and provide information about upcoming events. Sometimes
you can use these events to market your consulting services to
companies exhibiting at a job fair.

American Recruitment
www.americanrecruitment.com
888-44-FAIRS

Career Expo
www.careerx.com
513-721-3976

CFG Inc.
www.cfg-inc.com
402-697-9503

JobsAmerica
www.jobsamerica.com
408-748-7600

Lendman Group
www.lendman.com
800-288-2890

NAACP High-Tech and
Diversity Job Fairs
www.naacpjobfair.com
800-JOB-SHOW

National Career Centers
www.fayettevillenc.com/
nccjobfair/
800-326-9111

Agencies and consulting firms

The following firms primarily hire technology consultants (engineers, programmers, technical writers, software trainers, and so forth) and maintain multiple offices.

CDI Corporation
1717 Arch Street, 35th Floor
Philadelphia, PA 19103
215-589-2200
Fax 215-496-0799
www.cdicorp.com

Dashe & Thomson
401 North 3rd St., Suite 500
Minneapolis, MN 55401
612-338-4911
Fax 612-338-4920
www.dashe.com

IMI Systems
290 Broadhollow Road
Melville, NY 11747
516-425-7700
Fax: 516-425-7877
www.imisys.com

Manpower
World Headquarters
5301 North Ironwood
Milwaukee, WI 53217
414-961-1000
Fax 414-906-6188
www.manpower.com

New Boston Systems
50 Milk Street, 5th Floor
Boston, MA 02109
617-482-5200
Fax 617-482-2408
www.newboston.com

Renaissance (formerly
The Registry)
189 Wells Avenue
Newton, MA 02159
617-527-6886
Fax 617-527-6999
www.rens.com

Support Our Systems (SOS)
1 West Front St., 3rd Floor
Red Bank, NJ 07701
908-530-1800
Fax 908-530-1660
www.sosstaffing.com

Technisource
1901 W. Cypress Creek
Road, Suite 202
Fort Lauderdale, FL 33309
954-493-8601/800-940-1111
Fax 954-493-8603
Resume fax line:
888-290-2990
www.tsrc.net

TECH/AID
54 Jaconnet Street
Newton, MA 02161
617-244-8862 or 800-225-8956
www.techaid.com

Whittman-Hart L.P.
   311 South Wacker Drive, Suite 3500
   Chicago, IL 60606-6618
   312-922-9200
   Fax 312-913-3061
   www.whittman-hart.com

Fax services

Concord Technologies, Inc.
   2025 1ˢᵗ Avenue, Suite 800
   Seattle, WA 98121
   800-232-9269

Provides fax mailbox services. In addition, check with your local telephone company to see what fax mailbox services they may offer.

Sample Worksheets

Worksheet 1: Assessing your field

Use this questionnaire to assess how well your field supports consultants. For more information see Chapter 2.

Check the employment pages of your local newspaper. List below the names of any agencies placing ads for full-time or contract consultants.

_____

_____

List below any examples or samples of your work you can provide.

_____

_____

Does your field require any licenses? If so, list them below.

_____

_____

List any professional organizations appropriate for your field.

_____

_____

_____

List industry publications for your field.

_____

_____

_____

List any fields complementary to yours. For instance, training is complementary to human resources management.

_____

_____

Worksheet 2: Inventory your qualifications

Use this form to collect information about your qualifications to do consulting in your field. For more information, see Chapter 3.

How many years of experience do you have as a professional in your field?

_____

List awards you have won for your work.

_____

_____

_____

List clients or employers who have gone out of their way
to compliment your work.

_____

_____

_____

List your education.

_____

_____

_____

List any relevant professional or product certification
programs you have completed.

_____

_____

_____

List professional organizations you've joined.

_____

_____

_____

Worksheet 3: Business plan

Use this worksheet to help you build a plan for your consulting business. For more information, see Chapter 4.

Mission statement

Why are you doing this? _____

_____

_____

What do you want to do for your clients?_____

_____

_____

How do you measure quality? _____

_____

_____

What goals do you want to reach over and over again? _____

_____

_____

Strategy

What are your core services? _____

_____

_____

Generally, what makes your business different from the competition? _____

_____

_____

How do you intend to get the word out about your business? _____

_____

_____

Current status and future plans

Are you just starting out or have you been in business for a while? _____

_____

_____

Do you currently have clients? How many? _____

_____

_____

What do you hope to accomplish in the near future? _____

_____

_____

Where will/did you get the money to start your business? _____

_____

_____

Are you seeking outside funds to grow your business? _____

_____

_____

Market analysis

Is this market growing or contracting? _____

_____

_____

What statistics can you quote to support your analysis of the market's direction? _____

_____

_____

What does the market's direction mean for your business? _____

_____

_____

Niche

What part of the overall market will you focus on? _____

_____

_____

_____

What makes these market segments a good environment for your business?

_____

_____

_____

What services will you deliver to these market segments? _____

_____

_____

_____

Client profile

What kind and size of company buys your services? _____

_____

_____

What set of conditions creates the need for your services? _____

_____

_____

What kind of person is the decision maker? _____

_____

_____

How does the decision maker select an outside consultant with your services?

_____

_____

_____

Where would the decision maker look to find you? _____

_____

_____

Main features and benefits

What are the core, strategic features of your service? _____

_____

_____

Describe the benefits of these features to your target clients. _____

_____

_____

Describe how your service features differ from those of your competition.

_____

_____

_____

Competitive analysis

Provide an overview of your competition and the competitive environment.

_____

_____

_____

What are your competitive weaknesses? _____

_____

_____

Professional assets

Write a brief biography about your professional experience. _____

_____

_____

_____

_____

Worksheet 4: Cash flow estimator

Use this worksheet to estimate your cash flow as part of your business plan. For more information, see Chapter 4.

CASH FLOW FOR YEAR ___	Jan	Feb	Mar	Apr	May	Jun	Jul	Aug	Sep	Oct	Nov	Dec
STARTING CASH												
REVENUES												
Consulting												
Other												
TOTAL CASH ON HAND:												
CASH USES:												
MARKETING (take from Marketing Plan)												
OFFICE												
Supplies												
Postage												
Furniture												
Telephone												
Computer hardware												
Computer software												
BUSINESS INSURANCE												
General business liability												
Business property												
EMPLOYMENT												
Gross salaries												
Employer taxes												
Worker's Compensation insurance												
Health insurance												
Disability insurance												
Retirement plan												
BUSINESS FEES												
Incorporation franchise fee												
Local business fees												
PROFESSIONAL												
Membership fees												
Seminars/Conferences												
Training												
Publications												
TRAVEL												
Auto												
Hotel												
Meals												
Airfare												
OTHER												
TOTAL CASH USES:												
ENDING CASH:												

Worksheet 5: Setting your rate structure

Use this worksheet to estimate your rate and to create a rate strategy. For more information, see Chapter 5.

Rate estimator

Assumptions		Rates
Days in year*	180	Daily labor rate $_____ (Salary/days in year)
Salary	$_____	Daily overhead rate $_____ (Total overhead/days in year)
Profit margin	_____%	Daily profit $_____ (daily labor rate + daily overhead rate) * profit margin
Overhead: Expenses & benefits $_____ Retirement (15%) $_____		Daily billing rate $_____ (daily labor rate + daily overhead rate + daily profit)
Total overhead: $_____ (daily billing rate/hours in day)		Hourly rate $_____
Hours in day:	8	Gross yearly revenue $_____ (days in year * hours in day) * hourly rate
Hours in year:	1,440	Profit $_____ (Gross yearly revenue − salary − overhead)

* 365 days − 104 weekend days − 8 holidays − 10 vacation days − 5 sick days − 58 miscellaneous days for administration, marketing, and down time = 180 days

Rate strategy:

Estimated agency rate: _____

Direct rate for your clients: _____

Your wholesale rate: _____

Worksheet 6: Marketing inventory

Use this worksheet to inventory potential outlets to market your services. For more information, see Chapter 10.

List professional organizations to which you already belong or are planning to join, where you can network your services. Also note organizations that have directories or resource guides where you can market your service.

_____

_____

_____

List publications that are appropriate for advertising your service.

_____

_____

_____

List nonprofit organizations you care about, who might publicize your service in exchange for your sponsorship.

_____

_____

_____

List any colleagues or friends you can contact to start spreading the word about your consulting business.

_____

_____

_____

Write an outgoing voice mail message that advertises your business.

_____

_____

_____

_____

Worksheet 7: Marketing plan

Use this worksheet to outline your marketing plan. For more information, see Chapter 14.

Marketing plan for year _____

Marketing Methods		Cost	Timing												
Method	Implementation		Jan	Feb	Mar	Apr	May	Jun	Jul	Aug	Sep	Oct	Nov	Dec
P Directory Listings															
a Advertising															
s Mass Mail															
s															
i Publicity															
v															
e															
A Networking															
c Cold Calling															
t															
i Public speaking															
v															
e Seminars															
	Total Cost:														

Index

A

Accounting 151–158
  expenses 154–155
  flowchart 153
  IRS 151–154
  payroll 155–158
Adobe 32
Adobe Acrobat files 126
Advertising 25, 93-97
  on envelopes 110
  print 95
  Web page 94-95
  Yellow pages 95
Agencies and consulting firms 199–200
  independent consultants 13
  large consulting organizations 11-12
  list of agencies and consulting firms
    199-200
  marketing to 133-146
  noncompete clause 169-170
  rates 44-46
  small consulting businesses 13
Aldus PageMaker 7
Alta Vista 127
Amazon.com 127
American Bar Association (ABA) 24, 33
American Heritage Dictionary 8
American Medical Association (AMA)
  24, 33
Andersen Consulting 12
ASCII text 126
Assoc. of Systems Managers (ASM) 98
Attorneys 24, 55, 59, 75, 81, 145, 170

B

Bierce, Ambrose 67
Billing, methods of payment 53-54
Bookkeeping 151–158
  expenses 154–155
  flowchart 153
  IRS 151–154
  payroll 155–158
Brochures 113-114
Brokered consulting
  independent consultants 13
  large consulting organizations 11-12
  list of agencies and consulting firms
    199-200
  marketing to 133-146
  noncompete clause 169-170
  rates 44-46
  small consulting businesses 13
Burke, Edmond 35
Business and tax issues 55–65
  C corporations 61–62
  contract employees 56–57
  IRS definitions 62–65
    20 factors 62–63
    safe harbor 63–65
    section 1706 64–65

  partnerships 58–59
  S corporations 59–61
  sole proprietor 57–58
Business card, sample 113
Business plan, creation of 35–38
  components of 36–38
  example 39–42
  sample worksheet 203–206
  use of 35
Business resources 195–196

C

C corporation 55
C.E. Weekly 136
Campbell, Joseph 17
CARA 15
Career fairs, marketing at 100-102
Carnegie, Andrew 45
CD-ROM 88
Certified Network Engineer (CNE) 32
Checklist, new client preparation 177
Clients 173–178
  cold calling 102-105
  collecting information 173–178
  follow up 178
  maintaining information 173-176
  post-project survey, sample 179
  preparation checklist 177
  types of 21-23
  why they need consultants 19
  working with 176–178
Clough, Arthur Hugh 91
COBRA 68-69
Cold calling 102-105
Consulting firms and agencies 199–200
Consulting in specific fields 19–26
  assessment 23–26
  types of clients 21–23
    consulting to business 21–22
    consulting to consumers 22–23
    consulting to peers 22
  why needed 19–21
Consulting, overview 5–17
  benefits of 15–16
  categories of 9–11
    departmental outsourcing 11
    expert-advice consulting 10–11
      analysis 10
      project management 10
    skills contracting 10
  challenges to 16–17
  definition of 8–9
  paths leading to 5–8
  three main types of 11–13
    independent consultants 13–15
      career path of 13-15
    large consulting organizations 11–12
    small consulting businesses 13
Consumer Price Index (CPI) 70
Contract Professional magazine 45
Contracts 167–171

components 168–170
  cancellation 169
  compensation 168
  disputes 170
  hold harmless clause 170
  liability 170
  noncompete clause 169
  proprietary rights 169
  relationship of parties 168
  scope of work 168
  consulting an attorney 170
goals 167–168
sample contract 175
sources for 170
Corporate politics 16
Csikszentmihalyi, Dr. Mihaly 6

D

Data Processing Independent Consultants
  Exchange 137
Data Processing Managers Association
  (DPMA) 98
Deductions 57, 61-62, 88-90
Dickens, Charles 55
Directories 93, 97, 136, 148
Directory of Contract Service Firms 136
Directory of Independent Consultants 148
Directory of Technical Service Firms 136
Disability insurance 69–71
Doing Business As (DBA) 58
Dow Jones Industrial Average 44

E

EDI 12
80/20 rule 183
Eisenhower, Dwight D. 147
Emerson, Ralph Waldo 5
Errors and omissions insurance 74
Expenses 49-50, 57
  home office 89
  IRS definition 154-155
  record-keeping 151-154

F

Fax services 200
Federal Employer ID 58, 60
Figures
  payroll flowchart 157
  record-keeping flowchart 153
  sample business card 113
  sample business plan 39–42
  sample contact form 175
  sample letterhead 111
  sample live cold-calling script 105
  sample marketing plan 149
  sample post-project survey form 179
  sample proposal 163–166
  sample rate increase letter 51
  sample resume 116
  sample voice mail script 105
  sample Web page 120
Fitzgerald, F. Scott 181
Fixed bid 53-54

Follow-up
  post-project survey 178-179
Forster, E.M. 1, 27
Franklin, Benjamin 159

G

Government resources 195

H

Hall, Becky 160
Health insurance 68-69
Hendrick, Burton J. 45
Holtz, Herman 8
Home office set-up 83–90
  communications 84–86
  computer equipment 86–88
  home office, deducting 88–90
Hourly rate
  calculating 48-50
  categories of 44-47
  estimating 47-48
  lowering 52-53
  method of payment 53
  raising 50-52
  rate structure 43-54
HyperText Markup Language (HTML)
  8, 119
  editing programs 196

I

IBM 12
Illinois Institute of Technology 32
Incorporation 55, 59-62
  C corporation 61-62
  S corporation 59-61
Independent Computer Consultants
  Association (ICCA) 25, 64, 98, 171
Independent consultants 27–31
  qualifications 31–33
  traits of 27–31
Independent contractors
  IRS definition 62-65
  sole proprietor status 57
Insurance 67–74
  business 72–74
    equipment 73
    liability 72
    workers compensation 73
  disability 69–70
  errors and omissions 74
  health 68–69
  life 71–72
  personal benefits 67
Interface materials 109–118
  brochures 113–114
  business cards 112
    sample 113
  envelopes 110–112
  invoices and checks 117
  letterhead 110
    sample 111
  portfolios and pitch books 117–118
  resumes 115–116

Internet. *See* Marketing on the Web
Internet Job Boards 197–198
Internet Service Provider (ISP) 121
IRS 56–61, 151, 195
    Expenses for Business Use of Your
        Home (Form 8829) 89
    safe harbor 63-65
    section 1706 64-65
    20 factors 62-63
ISO 9000 21

J

James, Henry 119
Job fairs 198
Johnson, Samuel 151

K

Kintler, David 8
Kundera, Milan 109

L

Lawrence Berkeley Lab 20
Legal issues
    contracts *See Contracts*
    form of business 55-62
    limiting liability
        errors and omissions insurance 74
        through incorporation 60
Letterhead, sample 111
Limited Liability Corporation (LLC) 55
Lycos 127

M

Mailings
    letterhead 110
    follow up 178
    mass mailing 96
Manpower 15
Marketing on the Web 119–131
    associated links 127
    banner ads 130
    classified ads 131
    content 125–127
    domain name 124
    getting people 128–131
        search engines 128–130
            registering 128
            search-engine friendly 129-130
    Internet Service Provider (ISP) 121
    reciprocal links 131
    sample Web page 120
    Web site, homes 121
        current provider's system 121
        free host sites 121–124
            GeoCities 122
            Angelfire Communicaitons 123
            XOOM 123
            Tripod 123
            Webspawner 123-124
        Yellow pages 130
        your own Internet identity 124
Marketing plan, creating 147–150
    cost 148

implementation 148
    method 147
    sample plan 149
    sample worksheet 210
    timing 148
Marketing strategies 91–107
    active techniques 97–107
        career fairs 100–102
        cold calling 102–104
            sample script 105
        networking 98–100
        public speaking 104–106
        seminars and teaching 106–107
    passive techniques 93–97
        certified vendor listings 94
        cross-business promotions 97
        mass mailing 96
        membership directories 93
        nonprofit promotions 97
        print advertising 95
        referral bulletin boards 96
        resource guides 93–94
        Web page 94–95
        Yellow Pages 95
    principles, basic 92–93
Marketing, to agencies 133–146
    advantages of 134
    agency cycle 143–146
    cautions 141–142
    disadvantages of 134–135
    tips on 138–140
    where to find 135–138
        Internet 137
Marketing tools. *See* Interface materials
Masella, Candace 95
Medicare 56–59
Microcomputer Managers Association 98
Microsoft 32

N

NameSecure 124
National Association for the Self-Employed
    (NASE) 136, 193
National Technical Services Association
    (NTSA) 64
National Writers Union 171
Networking 25, 47, 98-100, 183
Niche, as part of business plan 37
1986 Tax Reform Act 64
Nolo Press 171
Noncompete clause 169-170
Novell 32

O

Office, setting up *See Home office set up*
Organizations, list of 192–194

P

PageMaker 7
Parker, Dorothy 83
Passos, John Dos 19
Payroll 20, 57
    agency saving 139-140

flowchart 157
paychecks for yourself 152
record-keeping 155-158
taxes on dividends 154
PD News 136
Periodicals, list of 194–195
Post-project survey form, sample 179
Power Builder 32
Professional organizations
    list of 192-193
    membership directories 93
    networking 98-100
  · referral bulletin boards 96
Proposals 160–162
    components 160–162
    sample 163–166
    writing 160
Public speaking 104-106

Q

Quark 32

R

Rate structure 43–54
    calculating 48–50
        sample worksheet 208
    categories of 44–47
        agency rate 44–46
        break even rate 46
        direct client rate 46
        wholesale rate 46
    charging less 52–53
    creating a strategy 50
    estimating rates 47–48
    payment billing 53–54
        fixed bid 53
        retainer 54
    raising your rate 50–52
    sample calculation 49
    sample rate increase letter 51
Record-keeping 151–158
    expenses 154–155
    flowchart 153
    IRS 151–154
    payroll 155–158
Renaissance Worldwide 15
Resume, sample 116
Retirement funding 75–81
    Individual Retirement Account 75–78
        Roth IRA 79
        Standard IRA (deductible) 76–77
        Standard IRA (nondeductible) 77
    Keogh 75, 80
    other retirement plans 83
    Savings Incentive Match Plan for
        Employees (SIMPLE) 75, 83–84
    Simplified Employee Pension (SEP)
        75, 79–80
    summary of plans 81, 84
RFPs 162
RTF documents 126
Ruhl, Janet 8, 45, 64, 109

S

Safe harbor 63-64
Salary, paying yourself 59, 61, 152, 155-158
Sales *See Marketing strategies*
Schedule C 57, 89, 154
S corporation 55
Section 1706 64-65
Section 530 64
Self-employment tax 57
Seminars 22, 25, 98-99, 106-107, 148
Shakespeare, William 133
Shenson, Howard 160
Skills, evaluating 27-33
Social Security 57, 59
Society for Technical Communication (STC)
    24–25, 148
Software Publishers Association (SPA) 98
Sole proprietorship 55-58, 78-79, 88, 152, 154
Special Interest Groups (SIGs) 25
Stoll, Clifford 20

T

Tables and charts
    sample calculation of profitable rate 49
    types of retirement plans 81
Taxes 55-65
    IRAs 76-79
    payroll 20, 152, 155-158
    and agencies 139
Tax Reform Act of 1986 65
Telemarketing *See Cold calling*
Toastmasters 91, 194
20 factors, IRS 62-63

U

Universal Resource Locator (URL) 121

V

Virgil 173
Voice mail script, sample 105
Voltaire 75

W

W-2 14, 59, 61, 65, 134, 140, 152, 158
Wang Laboratories 7
Web home page host sites 196–197
Web page, sample 120
Web search engines 197
Web site Missing Link 131
Withholding taxes, payroll *See Payroll*
Worksheets
    assessing your field 201
    business plan 203-206
    cash flow estimator 207
    inventory your qualifications 202
    marketing inventory 209
    marketing plan 210
    setting your rate structure 208

Y

Yahoo 127
Yellow pages advertising 95

Give the Gift of
Successful Independent Consulting
to Your Friends and Colleagues

CHECK YOUR LEADING BOOKSTORE OR ORDER HERE

❏ YES, I want _____ copies of *Successful Independent Consulting* at $17.95 each, plus $3 shipping per book (IL residents please add $1.21 sales tax per book). Canadian orders must be accompanied by a postal money order in U.S. funds. Allow 15 days for delivery.

My check or money order for $_____ is enclosed.
Please charge my ❏ Visa ❏ MasterCard

Name _____

Organization _____

Address _____

City/State/Zip _____

Phone _____

Card #_____ Exp. Date _____

Signature _____

Please make your check payable and return to:
Logical Directions, Inc.
PO Box 0357
Brookfield, Il 60513-0357

Call your credit card order to 800-507-BOOK (800-507-2665)
Fax 708-728-3768

12/99